William Hale Beckford

The Leading Business Men of Norwich and Vicinity

Embracing Greeneville and Preston

William Hale Beckford

The Leading Business Men of Norwich and Vicinity
Embracing Greeneville and Preston

ISBN/EAN: 9783337216115

Printed in Europe, USA, Canada, Australia, Japan

Cover: Foto ©Suzi / pixelio.de

More available books at **www.hansebooks.com**

Leading Business Men

NORWICH.

THE

LEADING BUSINESS MEN

OF

NORWICH

AND VICINITY,

EMBRACING

GREENEVILLE AND PRESTON.

ILLUSTRATED.

—

BOSTON:
MERCANTILE PUBLISHING COMPANY,
No. 258 Purchase Street.
1890.

PREFACE.

In this historical and statistical review of the commercial and manufacturing interests of Norwich, it has been our purpose in as thorough a manner as was possible to justly describe those enterprises which have contributed so largely during the last half century to the material advancement of the city. History plainly shows that many large cities owe their prosperity and growth chiefly to advantages of situation, great influx of foreign people, and similar causes; the present prosperity of Norwich, however, is due solely to the genius and efforts of its people. A study of these facts, and of its varied mercantile interests, which are presented herewith, must show clearly, we think, the rich harvests that have been reaped from the exertions and foresight of the past, the present flourishing and influential position of Norwich as a commercial center, and its bright outlook for many lines of growth in the time to come. In the review of the commercial and manufacturing interests of this section, it has been our purpose in as thorough a manner as was possible to justly describe those enterprises which have contributed so largely during the last half century to the material advancement of Norwich and Vicinity. We have made several extracts from the very complete volume issued by the Board of Trade in 1888, and are indebted to the secretary for the present list of members of the board.

MERCANTILE PUBLISHING CO.

[For Contents see last pages.]

NORWICH AND ITS POINTS OF INTEREST

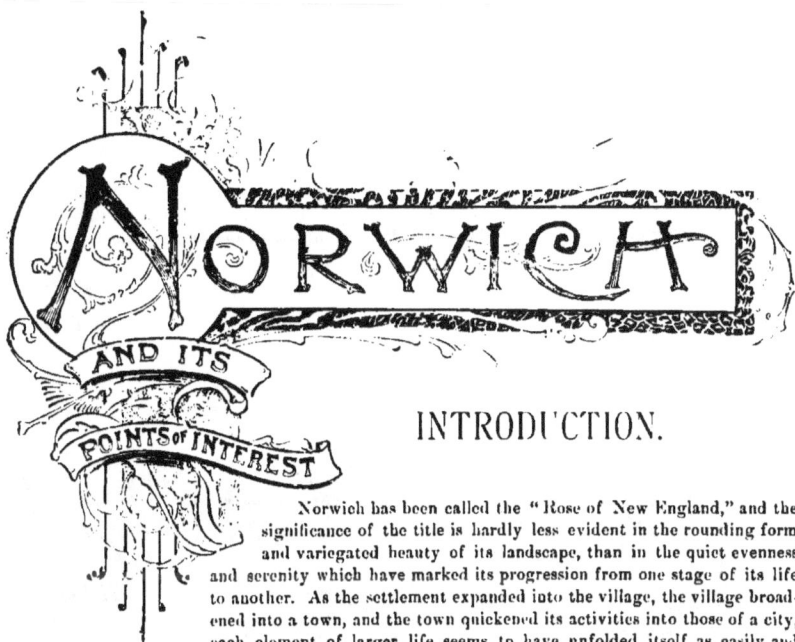

INTRODUCTION.

Norwich has been called the "Rose of New England," and the significance of the title is hardly less evident in the rounding form and variegated beauty of its landscape, than in the quiet evenness and serenity which have marked its progression from one stage of its life to another. As the settlement expanded into the village, the village broadened into a town, and the town quickened its activities into those of a city, each element of larger life seems to have unfolded itself as easily and imperceptibly as the petals of a flower. It is true it has shared somewhat the periods of temporary depression, and more the enthusiastic movements which have swept throughout the country, yet these influences have not sufficed to mar or check perceptibly the calm development of its internal life, which has flowed on rather with the steady, silent sweep of the Thames near its mouth, than like the rushing, noisy Shetucket circling among the hills. From the sensational standpoint, therefore, Norwich must be placed among those few and happy regions that appear to have little or no history, because it is unrelieved by points of glaring contrast or eminent calamity. No fiery devastation or deadly plague have drawn black, gloomy lines around pages of its life, nor have the "sweet security" of its streets and the sanctity of its homes ever been violated by a hostile foot. Nevertheless the study of its historic annals has deep and intrinsic interest for every thoughtful reader, presenting many of the great problems of human life and nature in new and suggestive lights. By the steadiness of the city's advance by gradual stages, the impression of its solidity and enduring strength is powerfully conveyed to one who will examine the foundations upon which this advance has

The aboriginal history of Norwich lays largely in that shadowy ground which is handed over to the poet, to people with the traditionary forms of prehistoric times. At the time the English first settled, there seemed to have been no tribe dwelling at this spot for many years. Evidences of an Indian race, probably closely allied to the Pequots, point to their occupation some time prior to the English advent, of the region about Chelsea Plain; but, scattered to the four winds by hostile neighbors, or wasted away by the silent hand of disease, they had left, for unknown years, this beautiful spot a seldom broken solitude. The Monhegans, tributary to the Pequots before 1637, had a wandering home at Yantic to which they sometimes resorted. Their main seat was further down the Thames, and after the destruction of the mighty Pequots in 1637 by the English under Captain John

NORWICH IN 1850.
From an old print.

Mason (the future founder of Norwich), the Monhegans held a general claim to all this region. In 1643 one of the most famous of Indian battles occurred near Yantic Falls, between the Narragansetts and the Monhegans. By a wily stratagem Uncas, the chief of the latter, totally routed the Narragansetts, one tradition being that a party of them was driven headlong over the precipice above the Falls, and dashed among the foaming rocks. Miantonomo, the great chief of the Narragansetts, was also captured at the spot now known as Sachem's Plain. Here a mound of victory was raised by the Monhegans, and after the questionable justice of the English had sanctioned the execution of the captured prince, his lamenting people, adding each a stone or two in memory of their vanquished chieftain in their frequent passings this way, made quite a large monument on this spot. Though this mound has been swept away with the years, a small granite monument erected here in 1841 by citizens of Norwich, perpetuates the remembrance of this early battle and its vanquished chief.

VIEW OF HARBOR, 1890.

THE EARLY SETTLEMENT.

Norwich is an offshoot of Saybrook. This seaport village was first established under John Winthrop, Jr., in 1635, and among its most prominent early settlers were Captain John Mason of Pequot fame and the Rev. James Fitch, its first minister. Captain Mason was the leader in movements resulting in the founding of Norwich, being joined by about half the settlers of Saybrook. In May, 1659, he obtained the privilege from the Colonial Court of setting up a new town in the Monhegan territory and in the following months by fair and square purchase the "Nine Mile Square" section, now Norwich, was purchased by the Saybrook pioneers. The sum of twenty pounds, for which the whole nine miles were transferred forms a striking contrast to the present value of real estate in Norwich, but was considered a "full and juste" equivalent by Uncas and his associates. The name of Norwich occurs in the original deed, and was undoubtedly given in honor of the English city of the same name; some of the prominent settlers being probably from that town. The complete and formal session of the land was made in August, 1659, and the first settlement made about that time. The "Town-plot" with the sole street of Norwich was laid out along the eastern bank of the Yantic. Here in close proximity the first citizens took house lots and built their first habitations. About the centre of the plot a space was set aside for a "Green," facing which the first meeting-house was erected soon after the settlement. Near it also stood the houses of the Rev. Mr. Fitch and Major Mason. Among the other authenticated first settlers were Thomas Adgate, Robert Allyn, William Backus, John Baldwin, John Birchard, Thomas Bliss, Morgan Bowers, Hugh Calkins, Richard Edgerton, Francis Griswold, Christopher Huntington, Simon Huntington, William Hyde, Samuel Hyde, Thomas Leffingwell, John Olmstead, John Pease, John Post, John Reynolds, Jonathan Royce, Nehemiah Smith, Thomas Tracy and Robert Wade. A mill for the grinding of the local crops, the prime essential of almost every new settlement, was erected first at "No-man's Acre," then removed below the Falls by John Elderkin within about a year after the settlement. The first child of Norwich, Elizabeth Hyde, was born in August, 1660.

The first years were marked by quiet, uninterrupted progress. There is no record of suffering from privation, and though rumors of Indian troubles in the north and east floated hither occasionally, and warlike parties sometimes passed near by, no lives seem to have ever been lost. The valuation of the town in 1663, four years after the settlement, was £2,571. The earliest town clerk was John Birchard, and among the first representatives in the town government and at the general court, were Thomas Leffingwell, Christopher Huntington, John Bradford, John Calkins, Thomas Tracy, Hugh Calkins, Francis Griswold. In 1675 and '76 the war with King Philip gave Norwich some glimpses of military life. The town contributed its quota of twenty men, and in the winter of '75 and '76 was the rendezvous for the colonial troops of this section. This was about as near to immediate military action as the town ever came. A new meeting-house, considerably larger than the old one and on the high hill above the "Green," was completed in 1676. In 1684 the valuation of the town had arisen to £6,265, and its taxable population to 115. In 1685 the right of the town to the original tract of nine miles square was confirmed by a new patent from the colonial legislature of Connecticut, and establishing the township on a firm legal basis. The town continued to grow slowly from now on to the end of the seventeenth century

THE EIGHTEENTH CENTURY.

Just before and around 1700, several neighboring townships, including Preston, Lebanon, Windham, Griswold, Plainfield, Canterbury, and Mansfield, were largely founded and maintained through the influence of Norwich. One of the most prominent men of Norwich and this part of Connecticut, at this time, was Major Fitch, who was of great service to the colony in the settlement of disputes with the Indians, and in arranging of land difficulties and surveys through this and other sections of the colony. One of the most important features of the early part of the eighteenth century in Norwich, was the progress of the dispute with New London over County honors. Norwich became a half shire town in 1734, wresting a part of the county court business from the hands of New London. About this time the first town house was erected together with a jail, in connection with the new court. The extent of its business may be inferred from the fact that during 1740 there were upwards of 550 actions on the docket. In those days the slightest offences were deemed worthy of a fine, smoking at the town meeting being subject to a penalty of five shillings. During the first half of this century two public plots or commons were set apart, one being near the centre of the town, and the other on Bean Hill. The value of these measures has been realized in later years ; as the town has grown around and beyond these public parks, their usefulness and beauty has become more evident.

Norwich early gave attention to educational matters, there being in 1745 as many as seven district schools scattered through the town. In the following year Benedict Arnold, at that time a resident of Norwich, being elected to the grand jury, refused to serve, an incident which from later develop-

VIEW FROM JAIL HILL.

ments suggests more than it must have done at the time. In 1751, owing to the annoyance caused by troublesome intruders, the selectmen of the town voted that no land should be sold to strangers, nor any stranger be allowed to stay in town without public consent. It is unnecessary to say that this antique and inhospitable attitude was long since thrown aside, the present city being well known for its generous hospitality. It was estimated in 1754 that Norwich was paying the highest tax of any township in the colony. Among the largest and most influential families of the town in the period prior to the Revolutionary war, were those of the following names : Abell, Backus, Bushnell, Edgerton, Huntington, Fitch, Hyde, Lathrop, Leffingwell, Perkins, Smith, Tracy, and Waterman.

During the middle of the eighteenth century there sprang up in Norwich a considerable interest in commerce, vessels being fitted out for Boston, New York, the West Indies, Nova Scotia, and even across the water to England. A number of prominent business enterprises were inaugurated at this time, including the mercantile houses the Lanman Bros., Trumbull, Fitch & Trumbull, Thomas Coit, Prosper Wetmore, and Gershom Breed. During the French wars of this period Norwich's share seems only to have been the occasional sending of men and supplies to the service, according to the quota allotted to it. In 1758 a regiment was raised at Norwich for the war, of which Samuel Coit, of this town, was colonel. Among other Norwich citizens who served in the French wars were Colonel

THE PARK CONGREGATIONAL CHURCH.

Eleazar Fitch, Colonel William Whiting, Captain Robert Denison, Captain Samuel Mott, Dr. Robert Denison, Dr. Philip Turner, and Elizah Huntington.

The great religious movement of this century, known as the "New Light," or "Great Awakening," made a deep impression upon Norwich, the three churches of the town entering heartily into the movement, though not sympathizing with some of the later extravagances to which it was carried. As the century wore on many of the old Puritanic severities were laid aside and social life became more free and jovial. Elections, training-days, and Thanksgiving were the times of special festivities, but dinners and parties also became quite frequent, and wedding-festivities were celebrated with considerable spirit, as the following notice of a wedding attended by many Norwich people, evidences :

"A great wedding-dance took place at New London at the house of Nathaniel Shaw, Esq., June 12, 1769, the day after the marriage of his son, Daniel Shaw, and Grace Coit ; 92 gentlemen and ladies attended and danced 92 jigs, 52 contra-dances, 45 minuets, and 17 horn-pipes, and retired at 45 minutes past midnight." This quotation shows that at this time dancing was not one of the lost arts.

In 1773 the first newspaper ever published in Norwich, the *Norwich Packet*, was established and conducted with great popularity by the firm of Robertson & Trumbull. A census taken in 1774 showed the population to be 7,321. The grand list for the following year was £66,678.29, making Norwich second only to New Haven in valuation of all the towns in the colony.

THE WAR OF INDEPENDENCE.

Norwich entered into the movements preceding the Revolutionary war with zeal and thorough determination. The Stamp Act in 1764 elicited a most decided outburst of indignation. The citizens burned the effigy of the stamp-master, Ingersoll, and a large body of them marched to New London, joining in a great demonstration against the Stamp Act. Frequent liberty-meetings were held in the town and the spirit of independence grew steadily. The militia of the town were trained to be ready for marching at any time, and in May, 1774, there were four companies here under the following captains : Jedediah Huntington,

CHURCH STREET.

Samuel Wheat, Isaac Tracy, Jr., Gershom Breed. In the autumn of this year a regiment was organized at Norwich, of which Jedediah Huntington was made colonel. The fact that the great war governor of Connecticut, Jonathan Trumbull, was connected with Norwich helped to make the unanimity with which her citizens supported him more prominent. The people were practically as one man in every movement for the advancement of the cause. The very few Loyalists here were conspicuous by their loneliness. A large number of Norwich's most active and prominent sons participated in the campaign of 1775 about Boston and throughout the war. Beside the officers already mentioned the following also served with distinction: Edward Mott, Samuel Gale, Josiah Baldwin, Elisha Lee, Asa Kingsbury, Major Durkee, Major Labdiel Rogers, Captains Joseph Jewett, Jacob and Joseph Perkins, Johnson, Stephens, Night, Waterman, Lathrop, Brewster, Leffingwell and McCall. A portion of the Norwich men fought gallantly at Bunker Hill, and a little later a body of militia were despatched to New London to help repel a marauding expedition of the British. Norwich was its central and interior location and was made the temporary home of quite a number of noted Tories and British captives who were sent here for safe keeping. Norwich furnished her full quota of men throughout the war and also a large amount of money and supplies. In the assault and burning of New London, September 6, 1781, Norwich despatched a large number of eager soldiers to repel the attack from one of her recreant sons. Owing to her inland position Norwich did not suffer from marauding expeditions at all and furnished a fine harbor of refuge for pursued vessels. After the first stress of the war had passed she did not suffer much from want, and in the last few years enjoyed exceptional prosperity, agriculture flourishing, and the foundations of her large manufacturing interests being laid. A number of Norwich men gained high honors in the naval service during the war, among these being Captains Lester, Robert Niles, Seth Harding, Timothy Parker, Henry Billings, Thomas Parker, Jabez and Hezekiah Perkins, William Wattles, Thomas King, Ebenezer Lester, William Loring, Jabez Lord and Elisha Lathrop. The privateering business was carried on from this port with great energy but with alternating good and bad fortune. Many of the vessels and crews were captured, many cargoes lost, but with steady intrepidity it was kept up to the last. Not a few glowing and brilliant narratives adorn the marine records of this period. The largest and most influential shippers in Norwich at this period were Howland & Coit, who maintained their mercantile business throughout the war. Sons of Norwich also won high recognition and authority in the land service. Among these was Major-General Jabez Huntington, who during the last half of the war had supreme command over the troops of the State; Major-General Jedediah Huntington, who commanded his troops with great efficiency at the battle of Long Island and other important engagements; Colonel Joshua Huntington; General Ebenezer Huntington, one of Washington's most reliable officers. It may be remarked in passing that hardly another family in the State or country can excel this Norwich family in its contribution of distinguished members of successive generations to the military service. Other able officers were also Colonel John Durkee, who fought with especial honors at Long Island, Trenton, and Monmouth; Colonel Benjamin Throop, Colonel Labdiel Rogers, Colonels Benajah and Christopher Leffingwell, Captain David Nevins, Captains Jedediah and James Hyde, Captain Simeon Huntington, Captain Elisha Prior, one of the Fort Griswold heroes, Captain Richard Lamb, Captain Andrew Lathrop, and Lieutenants Charles Fanning, Andrew Griswold, Silas Goodell, and Jacob Kingsbury. It is thus evident what a distinguished roll of honor Norwich had in the War of Independence, and this represents but a part of her gallant and devoted sons.

After the Revolution, for the balance of the century, the town continued to advance quietly but steadily. Norwich at this time covered a large extent of territory, and in 1786, without any heat or controversy, it was divided, three outlying sections being set apart as separate towns under the names of Lisbon, Bozrah, and Franklin. The West India trade of Norwich continued to grow through this period and into the next century. This city was intimately connected with New London, at this time not a few firms having connections in both and inter-partnerships. Christopher Leffingwell was the first naval officer of this port, appointed in 1784. Live stock, provisions, and lumber were among the most common articles of export, and even a considerable amount of flour was then raised here and shipped to the south. In 1788-89 the total value of the exports was £34,218, and of imports, £24,793, the balance of trade, according to the then prevalent theory, being greatly in Norwich's favor. The following shipping at that time belonged to this port :   Twenty sloops (940 tons), five schooners (325 tons), five brigs (545 tons), one ship (200 tons), in all, 2010 tonnage.   In the last decade of the eighteenth century the West Indian traders were much troubled by English and French men-of-war ships, those two countries being then at war, and preying on neutral nations, but nevertheless the Norwich commercial interests continued to grow.   In 1795 the tonnage of this port was almost twice what it had been six years previously : consisting of seven ships, nine brigs, nine schooners, and seventeen sloops, a total tonnage of 4,312 tons, this not including river and New York packets. After the first few years of the present century, trade with the West Indies rapidly declined, the depredations of the French and English war vessels being very severe, and after 1807, the Embargo adding another heavy burden.   The war of 1812 added the last straw, and the shipping of Norwich has never again seen the palmy days it enjoyed from 1783 to 1803.   A number of Norwich seamen were impressed by the British, and this added to the exasperation with which the town entered into the naval war from 1812 to 1815, which emancipated American shipping to a large extent, but was otherwise disastrous to the town's interests.

In the last part of the eighteenth century quite a number of Norwich citizens emigrated to the north, helping to found and settle towns in Vermont, New Hampshire, and Nova Scotia, the prospects there seeming inviting.   Chapman, Lathrop, Hyde, Harris, Tracy, and Post are some of the names of Norwich families transported to these.   Norwich, Vermont, owes its name to the fond memory of former citizens of this town, and Hyde Park, Vt., also received its name in honor of a Norwich citizen, Captain Jedediah Hyde.   Norwich, Mass., also was named after and in recollection of this place.   The people of this town also were active and prominent in the settling of the Wyoming Valley, and some of the victims who fell in the cruel slaughter there in July, 1778, were from Norwich families.   War- wick and Bedford, Pennsylvania, and other towns in western New York, Ohio and different parts of the west, owe their origin to this place, which was prolific in sending out enterprising colonists.   Nor- wich, New York, named in her honor, is another evidence of her spreading fame and influence.   The Western Reserve was quite largely taken up by Norwich people.   These are but partial evidences of the wide and powerful influence through the west exercised by Norwich, few of the eastern cities surpassing her in this great movement.   Among the famous of her western progeny was the Hon. Samuel Huntington, who left Norwich with his family in 1801 for Ohio, of which State he was after- wards governor.   Another Hon. Samuel Huntington of this distinguished Norwich family, won high honors in his native State, being a member of the first Continental Congress in 1775, serving as presi- dent of that body in 1779 and 1780, and afterward as governor of Connecticut from 1786 to his death in 1796.   Hon. Roger Griswold, who was governor of the State in 1811 and 1812, was a former resident of Norwich and died at his old home in 1812.   Another leading Norwich man, Aaron Cleaveland, deserves honor from having introduced into the Connecticut legislature in 1779 the first bill in favor of the abolition of slavery.   In 1790 the census of the town showed a population of 7,578, not much of an increase over twenty years before, but the division of the town and the depletions consequent on the Revolutionary war and western emigration, account for the fact.   The first lodge of Free Masons in Norwich, the Somerset, and one of the oldest in the State, was established here in 1794, since which time the order has continually increased in size and influence.   Washington's death in December, 1799, was commemorated in Norwich with appropriate services.

The churches of Norwich seem to have been particularly subject to fires, all the more noticeably since large conflagrations have been so infrequent in the town.   The first Congregational Church was burned to the ground in 1801, and an improved edifice begun on the same site in the same year.   The Second Congregational Church in Chelsea was almost entirely consumed by a fire in 1844, having suffered a previous severe conflagration in 1793 ; the Main Street Congregational Church was destroyed by one in 1854 ; and also the Baptist Church in Greeneville was burned in the same year.   With these exceptions Norwich has been remarkably free from conflagrations of any considerable extent.   The fine arrangement of its territory and the abundance of water are no doubt important factors in this desirable result.

THE NINETEENTH CENTURY.

During the war of 1812-15, enterprising citizens of Norwich engaged in privateering, but with no considerable success, as the fleets of the enemy were large and powerful and the blockade of the Sound very severe. A few swift-sailing vessels succeeded in breaking the blockade, but only three are recorded as getting in again in safety. The father of Commodore Oliver Perry, who gained great celebrity by the victory on Lake Erie in 1813, was a resident of Norwich, and so the latter's success attracted especial interest and rejoicing. A regiment was drafted at Norwich during this war and served largely on the coast to defense. Several companies were dispatched from Norwich to the American army on the Canadian frontier, and these fought gallantly at the battles of Chippeway, Bridgewater, and Lundy's Lane. In the last battle Captain Joseph Kinney, of Norwich, fell on the field mortally wounded, after a valiant career. Among other Norwich men who gained distinction in this war were Colonel Elisha Tracy, Major George L. Perkins, and Captain J. Bates Murdock.

LAUREL HILL.

The war of 1812 culminated the influences which crippled the shipping interests of Norwich, the energies and inventiveness of her citizens were turned in other directions, and from this time we note the rise and progress of the manufacturing interests. One of the earliest enterprises was the manufacturing of nails, but in the interval from 1813 to 1816, the manufacture of cotton and woolen goods, the interest which has since developed so largely, was begun here. One of the most important events in the first half of the century was the arrival of the first steamboat in 1816. On October 16th of that year, Captain Bunker sailed up the Thames to Norwich on the *Connecticut*, the first steam-propelled vessel that had ever plied the Thames. The occasion was one of great excitement and re-joicing, and marked the opening of a new commercial era, namely, that of steam. In the following year a Norwich engineer, Gilbert Brewster, constructed a small steamer, the *Eagle*, the first one owned at this port, and July 1, of that year, the *Eagle* made its first trip down the river, meeting on its way the steamboat *Fulton*, Captain Law, which, with flags afloat and resounding music, was

THE SLATER MEMORIAL.

conveying President Munroe up the Thames on his tour of the United States. Just as the passengers of the *Eagle* were saluting the *Fulton* a terrific explosion occurred in the boiler, sweeping part of it through the cabin and out at the back of the boat. If any of the party had remained below they would have met an instantaneous death, but happily all were on deck. Barring this accident, this was the most auspicious occasion ever witnessed up to that time on the Thames, and not surpassed in interest for the people by anything since, not excepting the famous annual races. A regular steamboat line between Norwich and New York was opened in 1817, the *Connecticut* and *Fulton* constituting the service, and landings being made at New Haven and New London. Three trips were made each week. At a later date the *H. E. Eckford* was put on the route, under command of Captain Denison, who afterward commanded the *Fanny*. The *General Jackson*, Captain W. W. Coit, *Maria*, Captain Euclid Elliot, and the *Norwich*, *Huntress*, and *Worcester* were also well known boats on this line. Another mode of transportation which has had an incalculable influence in the upbuilding of Norwich, was first broached here on the formation of the Norwich & Worcester Railroad Co., in 1832; separate charters being obtained from the Legislatures of Connecticut and Massachusetts, the two parts of the company were united in 1836, with an aggregate capital of $1,700,000. The work on the road was begun November 18, 1835, and completed through to Worcester in March, 1840, a distance of fifty-eight miles, eighteen of which are in Massachusetts. The project was largely the result of Norwich men's efforts, and it furnished a powerful stimulus to local commercial interests, connecting Norwich to the West by rail via the Boston & Albany at Worcester. By the junction of this road with the New London & Northern, in 1853, another valuable outlet for the city's commerce was afforded. The steamboat traffic on the line between Norwich and New York was not unattended by disasters, as the sad fate of the *Atlantic* and the *Commonwealth* testify, but its importance steadily grew until a daily line became necessary. The present Norwich line with its large fleet, including the *City of Worcester*, *City of Boston*, *City of New York*, *City of Lawrence*, and *City of Norwich*, is one of the best known and most efficient lines on the Sound.

The city of Norwich had received its city charter during Revolutionary days in 1781, being one of the first five incorporated cities of the State. In 1825, the grand list of the city which had been $1,797,879, in 1800, had increased to $2,200,000. In 1850 it had more than doubled, being $4,446,480. In 1833, in accordance with a petition to the legislature, the northern section of the city was divided off, and since then its limits have included Chelsea, Greeneville and the Falls. A town house was erected at the cost of $9,000 in 1829, which has since been replaced by a more elegant structure. The Norwich Gas-Light Company was incorporated in 1853, and consolidated with a new company called the City Gas Company in 1858.

CITY HALL.

The Otis Library was incorporated in 1851. This beneficent city institution was created by the generosity of Joseph Otis, a merchant of Norwich, who gave it just about $10,500, in the erecting and furnishing of the building, and the first purchase of books. In his will he left a fund of $6,500, the income of which was to be expended in the purchase of new books, and a valuable collection has gradually been accumulated here. The building was completed in 1850. In 1865 there were 6,660 volumes in the library, which had been increased in 1888 to 15,000 volumes, and the fund at that time was $20,000.

The Norwich Free Academy, one of the best institutions of its kind in the country, grew out of a movement among the people of Norwich, inaugurated by the Rev. John P. Gulliver in 1850. The academy received an incorporation charter in 1854, on the petition of Russell Hubbard, William P. Greene, William A. Buckingham, and William Williams, who were among the largest of the original contributors to the fund of $100,000, to which forty persons contributed, and which formed the foundation of the academy. The main building was completed in 1856, at a cost of $35,000. The Peck Library was the gift of Mrs. Harriet Peck Williams, and named in honor of her father, Captain Bela Peck. It was originally stored in the main building, but was removed to the Slater Memorial Hall on its completion, and now numbers over 6,000 volumes, forming a very choice collection. The original fund of $5,000 has increased considerably from its beginning. In 1859, the academy received the gift of a house and grounds for the principal, from Mrs. Wm. P. Greene. Among the presidents of its board of trustees have been the Hons. Russell Hubbard, Wm. P. Greene and William Williams. The first principal of the school was Mr. Elbridge Smith, who conducted it from 1856 to 1865; he was succeeded by the Rev. Wm. Hutchison, and the latter gentleman in 1885 by Dr. Robert P. Keene who has since directed the interests of the school. The beautiful Slater Memorial Hall, under the charge of the Free Academy, is probably the finest building in Eastern Connecticut, and was erected

in honor of John F. Slater, by his son, Wm. A. Slater, and by him presented to the academy. It contains, besides the Peck Library and some other collections, one of the best and largest art collections in New England, containing many gems of sculpture and painting arranged with rare æsthetic taste.

A great celebration occurred in Norwich at the commemoration of its two-hundredth birthday, September 7 and 8, 1859. A grand military parade, a grand dinner and ball, and four valuable discourses and orations by Daniel C. Gilman, Hon. John A. Rockwell, Bishop Alfred Lee, and Donald G. Mitchell, were a part of the celebration, which surpassed anything previously of this nature in Norwich or Eastern Connecticut. Governor Wm. A. Buckingham of Norwich presided over the meetings, and General David Young was chief marshall. Ex-President Fillmore was among the honored guests. The four distinguished speakers were all natives of the town, whose glory and charm as well as noble history and fame were thus most fittingly commemorated. During the middle of the century the manufacturing interests of the city were carried quietly but uninterruptedly

MAIN STREET FROM POST OFFICE.

forward. Among the most important lines which were inaugurated or expanded were those of iron-milling, pottery, stocking-looms, paper, clocks and watches, cotton and woolen mills; also hemp, corks, oil and fire-arms. Some of the largest companies of the city and State were established at this period. Norwich has had an exceptionally distinguished series of mayors. The first mayor elected in 1784 was Benjamin Huntington, afterward judge of the Superior Court of Connecticut, and a member of the Continental and Constitutional Congress. He was succeeded by John McLaran Breed, 1796; Elisha Hyde, 1798; Calvin Goddard, 1814 (also member of Congress and judge of the Supreme Court); James Lanman, 1831; Francis A. Perkins, 1834; Charles W. Rockwell, 1835; Charles J. Lanman, 1838; Wm. C. Gilman, 1839; John Breed, 1840; Wm. P. Greene, 1842; Gurdon Chapman, 1843; John Breed, 1845; Charles W. Rockwell, 1846; John Dunham, 1847; Wm. A. Buckingham, 1849; Lafayette S. Foster, 1851; Erastus Williams, 1853; Wm. S. Brewer, 1855; Wm. A. Buckingham, 1856; Amos W. Prentice, 1858; James S. Carew, 1860; James Lloyd Greene, 1862 and throughout the Civil War. Besides other distinguished offices held by Norwich men during this period already mentioned, James Lanman was United States Senator from 1819 to 1825; Jabez W. Huntington,

Member of Congress from 1829 to 1834, and United States Senator from 1840 to 1841 ; John A. Rockwell, member of Congress from 1845 to 1849 ; Lafayette S. Foster, United States Senator from 1855 to 1865, in which year he served as president *pro tem.* of the Senate. Not a few sons of Norwich also served in Congress as representatives from other States. These names furnish but a partial idea of the honors the town has won through its sons in public and national life, in which she has always shown great powers. Among the most prominent lawyers of Norwich in the period preceding the civil war were the Hon. Henry Strong, James Stedman, Joseph Williams, George Perkins, John T. Adams, Lafayette S. Foster and John T. Wait. Among the most prominent physicians of the period

MAIN STREET FROM CORNER SHETUCKET STREET.

were Dr. Alfred E. Perkins, Dr. Philip Turner, Dr. John P. Fuller, Dr. Worthington Hooker and Dr. Wm. P. Eaton. Among the great mercantile leaders were Thomas Mumford, Joseph Howland, John Howland, Thomas Coit, Jacob Dewitt, Joseph Williams, Lynde McCurdy, Giles Buckingham, William Williams, Geo. L. Perkins and Wm. A. Buckingham. The last named was one of the most famous of Norwich's citizens, serving the State and country with marked ability and untold influence throughout the dark years of the war. He was first elected in 1853 and served for nearly ten years, being re-elected each time with increased majorities. To his example, far-seeing measures, and wise intrepidity, Connecticut owes not a small share of the honor she obtained in her steadfast and powerful support of the Union in the great struggle.

THE CIVIL WAR.

The people of Norwich were prepared by a deep and earnest sympathy which grew stronger each year, for the struggle against slavery, and when the news of the fall of Fort Sumter came April 14, 1861, responded with immediate and hearty zeal. They knew the character of their fellow citizen, Governor Buckingham, and answered his first appeal for volunteers within a few hours. Norwich was

CLUB HOUSE.

represented in the First Connecticut Regiment, which was organized at Hartford, April 16th, and of which Daniel Tyler, a resident of Norwich, was appointed colonel. For the next two regiments Norwich furnished three companies under the command of Captains Frank S. Chester, Henry Peale and Edward Harland. Lieutenant-Colonel David Young and Sergeant-Major John L. Spalding were also from this town. Within three months twelve commissioned officers and one hundred and thirty-five enlisted men had been furnished by Norwich. All of her representatives were engaged in the battle of Bull Run, where the Connecticut regiments saw some of the hardest service, but only one Norwich man, David C. Case, was killed, three being taken prisoners.

Fresh calls for troops issued in May and July, 1861, and July and August, 1862, were responded to immediately and full quotas sent out, with contributions of money and supplies. Norwich furnished one hundred and thirty-seven officers to the service during the war, including three generals (Tyler, Birge and Harland), five colonels, seven lieutenant-colonels, eight majors, eight adjutants, seven surgeons, forty-five captains and fifty lieutenants, a record equalled by but few cities. For the three months' service Norwich furnished one hundred and forty-eight men; for cavalry and artillery service, forty-two men; for three years infantry service, five hundred and twenty-eight enlisted men; for nine months' service, one hundred and twenty-six men; recruits, substitutes and colored men, about three hundred and fifty; as volunteers and substitutes in naval service, eighty-nine men, making a total of 1,260 men in the service. Edward Harland, of Norwich, went out in 1861 as colonel of the Eighth Connecticut Volunteers and led his regiment with great valor at the fierce battles of South Mountain and Antietam, in August, 1862, being promoted to a brigade command in the latter battle. Lieutenant

Marvin Wait, of the Eighth, fell in this battle while fighting valiantly, the first commissioned officer from Norwich slain on the field. Norwich had companies or parts of companies in the Ninth, Eleventh, Thirteenth (Colonel Henry W. Birge, from Norwich), Fourteenth, Twenty-First and Twenty-Sixth Connecticut volunteer regiments, but the Eighteenth Connecticut Volunteers was considered peculiarly the *home regiment*, being largely officered and manned, as well as recruited here. Among its Norwich officers were Col.

A WINTER VIEW ON RIVER.

onel William G. Ely, Sergeant-Major J. P. Rockwell, Quartermaster D. W. Hakes, Surgeon C. M. Carleton, Captains Davis, Bromley, Hakes, Peale and Knapp. The regiment left Norwich on August 22, 1862, and served with distinction at Winchester June 13th, 14th, 15th, 1863, where they suffered very severely, a large number being slain, and nearly half the regiment, including the colonel, being taken prisoner. The Eighteenth again fought gallantly at New Market, May 15, 1864, at Piedmont, Lynchburg and the second battle of Winchester during the latter part of the same year, and were mustered out at Harper's Ferry, June 27, 1865. General Howland served as brigadier-general and commandant in North Carolina through the last part of the war and commanded a division in the last fight of that section at Kingston, March, 1865. General Birge won distinguished honors for services

WASHINGTON STREET, NORWICH.

at Port Hudson, 1863, and in the Shenandoah Valley campaign of Sheridan in 1864. Commodore Joseph Lanman of the United States naval service was a native of Norwich. Warrington D. Roath, Robert B. Smith, and John W. Bentley of Norwich also commanded vessels in the marine service.

The Soldier's Aid Association of Norwich was very active and generous throughout the war, sending many useful and valuable gifts to the soldiers on the field and helping in the care of their families. The news of the surrender of Lee reached Norwich, April 10, 1865, and was followed by a celebration of guns, bells and general rejoicing. But four days later the news of President Lincoln's assassination turned the joy to mourning, and solemn religious services in his honor were held at Norwich on the 19th of April, and the following Sunday. The participation of the soldiers in the celebration of 4th of July, 1865, added a new and significant feature to the day, Generals Birge and Harland being among the veterans who were present. Over one hundred and forty sons of Norwich fell in the struggle, among whom were Lieutenant Chas. A. Breed, Lieutenant Alfred M. Goddard, Lieutenant Edward P. Manning, Captain Joseph H. Nickerson, Lieutenant Hervey F. Jacobs, Captain John McCall, Captain Jas. R. Nickles, Lieutenant Frederick G. Shalk, Lieutenant Marvin Wait and Corporal Frederick S. Ward, the last two being under twenty. In honor of her gallant and heroic sons who fell during the war of the Rebellion, Norwich has erected a beautiful monument.

Since the Civil War, the progress of Norwich has not been marked by any extraordinary events. The city suffered the general results felt throughout the country in the panic of 1873, but in spite of hard times the commercial interests of the city have advanced continually forward. The contents of the following pages will show that the superstructure raised in the present generation is not unworthy the foundations laid in earlier times. In 1885 the valuation of the city showed a total wealth of nearly $30,000,000, and this has been considerably increased in the intervening years. The population which in 1870 was 16,653, had increased in 1880 to 21,143, and is now estimated to be about 25,000, placing the city among the first four of the State. From its uniquely advantageous situation, fine resources, and the talents and character of its people, it cannot fail to far exceed in the future the progress of the past, and for a review of the present, showing the beauties and attractions of the Rose City as a manufacturing and educational center, and also as a place of residence, we welcome the reader to the following pages.

NORWICH AS A PLACE OF RESIDENCE.

Probably no city in New England is more picturesquely situated, or more attractive in its varied beauties, than is Norwich. Lying between sheltering hills, watered by the Thames, Shetucket, Yantic and Quinnebaug rivers, shaded from the heat of summer by lordly elms, oaks and maples, it excites the admiration and delight of all visitors, and has gained for itself the notoriety of being the most charming city in New England. It is the city and country combined. Stroll through Washington Street and Broadway, and view the beautiful private residences on either side of those charming thoroughfares. Where is their equal in outward elegance, or picturesque surroundings? Rest, for a moment in your stroll, at Williams Park, the *plaza* of the city, encircled, as it is, by fine elms and more of the beautiful residences which have made Norwich famous. A short distance to the east is a background of wooded hills; and to the west, an open, undulating country, with vistas of forests, farm houses and streams of flowing water. Near by, and facing the park, is the handsome Slater Memorial building, the Free Academy and Park Church, which have been elsewhere mentioned. From the upper end of the Park, and near the fine Soldier's Monument, take the street that leads to Norwich Town, a mile or more distant, which was the original settlement long before there was a building where the city now stands. Here, perched upon a high, rocky cliff in the rear of the present church edifice, the first church was built by the early settlers—built high, and almost inaccessible, with a stockade around it to protect the building and the worshipers from the sudden onslaughts of the wily savages. It required a good amount of courage to attend church in those days, for there was likely to be danger lurking behind every rock and forest tree. The brave church-goers religiously carried their rifles with them, and during divine service armed sentinels were stationed outside to guard against sudden attteks.

In this old town lived the Huntingtons, the Hydes, the Fitches, the Clevelands, the Masons, the Tracys, and scores of others of honored memories, whose ashes have long since mingled with the dust. Near the village green Mrs. Sigourney grew up from childhood amid the romantic scenery, the beauty of which she afterwards loved so dearly to recount in verse and prose. Times have changed wonderfully since those days; the public buildings have either been torn down, or changed into modern

EAST MAIN STREET.

FRANKLIN SQUARE, FROM EAST MAIN STREET.

dwelling houses; and with the exception of some very old gabled roof shops, there is little to remind one of the past. Standing upon the high rocks in the rear of the church, on a pleasant summer afternoon, one could imagine himself surveying the happy valley of Rasselas, so dreamy is the prevailing quietness, so gentle and noiseless the flow of the shining river as it winds and curves through the green meadows below.

Returning to Williams Park by the northerly street, you pass the grand old mansion, once the residence of Gen. Jedediah Huntington a century ago, and where he entertained Washington in the dark days of the Revolution.

Eastward of this, at the turn of the street southward, is a plain, unpretentious house, the birthplace of Lydia H. Sigourney, and where she passed her childhood days. A mile or more south of this is pointed out the spot on which the house stood where Benedict Arnold was born, and passed his younger days. The house was demolished many years ago, and nothing remains to remind one of this famous character—famous as a soldier, as well as a traitor,—but the old well and the curb that encloses it.

Arriving once more at Williams Park, turn down Sachem Street, you come to a place of great historical, as well as local interest, the grave of Uncas. The last resting place of this warrior and chief of the Mohegan tribe is romantically situated in a small grove by the wayside, and is surrounded by the graves of many of his red descendants. A plain granite shaft, bearing the simple name UNCAS on the base, covers the ashes of him who was a monarch with his tribe, and whose authority extended over the country far and near. The corner-stone of the monument was laid by President Jackson, in 1833; but the monument was not raised until 1842, when the ladies of Norwich completed the work which had remained so long unfinished. Further down the street is a pretty, rural cottage, which will long be known and pointed out as having once been the home of Donald G. Mitchell, and where, under the *nom de plume* of "Ik Marvel," he wrote two of his best works—Reveries of a Bachelor, and Dream Life.

Still further west, taking either of the two short streets which lead in a southerly direction, you come to the Falls Village, which derives its name from what was once a romantic cascade, formed by the waters of the Yantic wildly plunging through a

FRANKLIN SQUARE, FROM COR. SHETUCKET STREET.

narrow, rocky channel from a height of about forty feet. In years gone by, "The Falls" was a famous resort for all strangers visiting the city, thousands being attracted to it by the wildness of the scenery, the rushing, roaring waters covered with white foam, together with the old legends connected with the locality, especially that of a band of Indians, while being pursued by their enemies, jumping from the overhanging precipices into the boiling, seething waters below—a doubtful legend, to be sure, of Indian history, but of sufficient plausibility to give the place a weird and romantic interest. But what was known as "The Falls" of former days exists no longer in its original beauty and wildness, except it may be at times in the winter or spring, when the heavy rains and melting snows bring down vast bodies of water that come "tumbling and rumbling, and pouring and roaring like the waters of Lodore." The waters that once through all months of the year rushed madly down the rocky cascade, have been, in part, diverted through artificial channels to the great mills below, where they waste their strength in driving acres of machinery. The old rustic wooden bridge which spanned for so many years the roaring waterfall, and from which so many youths and lovers by moonlight and starlight have gazed upon the foaming waters beneath, has been removed by ruthless hands, and there is but little that now remains to connect the romance of the past with the business realities of the present.

Among the many beautiful drives and walks in and about Norwich, let the stranger not fail to visit Laurel Hill. Cross the fine iron bridge over the Shetucket from the eastern terminus of Water street, and take the road that borders, and in many places nearly overhangs the river, for two or three miles, in the direction of Poquetannoc. No view on the Hudson is more romantic or charming. As you pass over Laurel Hill, its streets bordered by elegant houses, and surrounded by tasteful and well-kept lawns, a beautiful panorama presents itself. Far below you the river Thames stretches its blue waters lazily towards Long Island Sound, while nearly beneath your feet, as it were, and within stone's throw, lies the business part of the city. It was but a few years ago that Laurel Hill was a wild tract of hilly, mountainous land, covered with laurels, rocks, wild cedars and brush ; a crooked cart path leading over it, and scarcely an indication that it was ever under cultivation, or even inhabited, if we may except a very old wooden farm house that still stands in the background of the main avenue as a relic of the past. Within a few years, this pleasant suburb has been constantly and largely increasing, and promises eventually to rival in importance the older portions of the city as a place of residence.

Let the stranger, while in Norwich, be sure to visit Taftville, and see the mammoth Ponemah Mills, which are mentioned in another part of this book. The short journey will well repay the trouble. It is a pleasant drive to pass through the manufacturing suburb of Greeneville, with its long array of mills and store-houses that line the river's banks. About a mile above, he comes to Sachem's Plain. Pause here a moment. In the open field yonder, on slightly elevated ground, is a square block of granite, on the base of which is carved the name of MIANTONOMOH, placed there to mark the spot where this celebrated Indian chief was slain by his bitter enemy, Uncas. A mile further, he comes to Taftville, and the enormous mill springs up before him as if by magic, and there seems to be no end to the vast pile of bright red brick and countless windows that reach into the far distance, like giants' castles in childhood's dreams. If there is time, go inside the mill, and take a glance at the acres and acres of moving machinery, and hear the hum, the whirr, and the rattle of wheels, and looms, and cards, and the one hundred and twenty-five thousand spindles, operated by fifteen hundred men, women and children.

Returning to the city, take the road to the left, and pass over Plain Hill and Waweens Hill, one of the most delightful drives in the State—the high altitude enabling you to get a magnificent view of the country far and near. Here you see fine farm houses and farming lands bordering the highways, villages here and there nestling among the forest covered hills ; and occasionally you catch a glimpse of the river Thames as it flows southward, and empties its waters into Long Island Sound.

FAIRVIEW RESERVOIR, NORWICH WATER WORKS.

CITY WATER SUPPLY.

No city in New England has a more abundant supply of good, wholesome water than Norwich. The reservoir, which covers sixty-six acres, being one and one-eighth miles long and an average width of 480 feet, is situated on high, elevated ground in the northerly part of the town, two and one-half miles from Franklin Square, the centre of the city. At this point the level of the overflow at the dam is 234 feet, and at tide water 253 feet, thus giving it a pressure or head that makes it of inestimable value as an auxiliary to our fire department in extinguishing fires. The reservoir gets its supply from natural springs that flow into it from the surrounding hills, and a water-shed of upwards of 400 acres. It has a capacity of 350,000,000 gallons, and by a small outlay can be made to hold a much larger amount should future demands require ; but, at present, the supply is fully adequate to the wants of a city twice the size of Norwich. The water from the reservoir is conducted as far as the Soldiers' Monument, at the head of Williams Park—a distance of one and one-half miles—in two mains, one 16-inch and one 14-inch. From this point water is distributed through smaller pipes to all parts of the city, including Greeneville, Laurel Hill, Thamesville and the Falls village. At the present time the water is supplied to 3,277 families, 815 offices and stores, 259 livery and private stables, 318 garden hydrants and hose, 287 public fire hydrants, 20, fire cisterns, 16 school-houses, 22 fountains, 41 steam engines, 62 manufactories, 230 street front sprinklers, 45 saloons, 26 markets, 25 green-houses and graperies, 9 fire-engine houses, and for a large number of other purposes.

The distribution of 287 fire hydrants throughout the streets of the city, and the pressure of a 250-feet head, makes the city almost safe against a fire of any magnitude. With such a force of water from a fountain head of such large capacity, in connection with our efficient fire department, Norwich virtually insures itself against the devouring element. Hose attached to one of the hydrants will easily throw a stream over the highest buildings in the city.

SEWERS AND SEWERAGE.

It is difficult for any city or town to obtain good sewerage where it is built on land that has an almost level surface. In such localities sewers may be, and are constructed, and if they do their work at all, they do it sluggishly, and to little or no purpose. Water will not flow naturally unless moved by the impetus of a downward tendency. Many of our New England, as well as our Western cities, suffer from having been built on plain lands, where it is impossible to get good drainage, and, in consequence, are visited periodically with fevers, epidemics and contagious diseases. All of the great scientists of the present day, and those among the medical fraternity who have made the origin of various diseases and epidemics a special study, unite in affirming that a large majority, even if not all epidemics and scourges which sweep off its victims by the hundreds and thousands—often designated as "visitations of God,"—are attributable to the want of sewerage, or to imperfect sewerage. As an instance in support of this conclusion, the case of Memphis, Tennessee, is referred to, which was almost depopulated a few years ago by yellow fever. Here, on account of the even surface of the land on which Memphis is built, no public or private sewerage had ever been attempted ; but when the dreaded scourge had almost wasted itself for the want of more victims to feed upon, the remnant of inhabitants awoke from their lethargy, and at an enormous expense and debt to the city, constructed sewers, with artificial flowage, which have seemingly had the effect of averting a repetition of the epidemic.

Happily, Norwich is so situated that it needs no artificial means to force running water through its sewers, or to wash its streets and gutters like Paris, and many cities which could be mentioned. Nature takes this work upon herself in our city, and often, after heavy rains and freshets, does it too lavishly. The streets lined with beautiful residences, warehouses and public buildings, rising one above another, are built on lands that rise abruptly from the rivers' banks that almost enclose the city, thus giving a natural and almost effective drainage. In connection with what nature has done in this respect, Norwich has built within a few years nine and one-half miles of sewers, at an expense of $100,000, through its principal streets, which empty themselves in a rapid current into the river. Vital statistics testify that there is no city in New England more healthy than Norwich, or one that is more free of epidemics of every kind, malaria, fevers or fever and ague.

Five years ago, 5,111 feet (a trifle less than a mile) of sewers were built in the streets of Greeneville, at an expense of $30,552.64, thus making that thrifty manufacturing suburb of the city a healthy, as well as a pleasant place of residence.

NORWICH POST OFFICE.

The following statistics, showing the business done at the Norwich Post Office during the year ending December 31st, 1889, have been kindly furnished by Postmaster Carruthers.

RECEIPTS POSTAGE ACCOUNT.

Received from stamps, envelopes, etc.	$29,360 43	
Received from box rents	1,380 75	
" waste paper	4 73	
		$30,645 91

EXPENSES

Postmaster's salary	$2,700 00	
Clerks' "	3,700 00	
Rent, light and fuel	2,224 63	
Miscellaneous	242 40	
Free delivery carriers, etc)	7,907 56	
		$16,774 59
Net income to department		$13,871 32

MONEY ORDER BUSINESS.

Balance on hand January 1, 1889	$251 59	
Domestic orders issued	44,088 42	
Postal notes "	4,412 35	
International orders issued	6,669 27	
Fees for domestic orders	363 75	
" postal notes	79 23	
" international orders	93 00	
Transferred from postage account	587 00	
		$56,544 61

Domestic orders paid	$42,452 08	
Postal notes "	4,024 80	
International orders paid	1,065 23	
Amount repaid	314 73	
" remitted by draft	8,485 00	
Balance on hand December 31, 1889	202 77	
		$56,544 61

REGISTRY DEPARTMENT.

Number of letters and packages registered	3,585	
Number of letters and packages received	3,729	
Number of letters and packages in transit	4,293	
		11,607

LETTER CARRIERS' DEPARTMENT.

Carriers employed	10
Delivery trips daily	4
Collection "	8

Registered letters and packages delivered	1,552	
Letters delivered	663,028	
Postal cards delivered	79,703	
Newspapers, etc., delivered	515,662	
Letters collected	402,044	
Postal cards collected	64,483	
Newspapers, etc., collected	44,400	
		1,770,872

BOX AND GENERAL DELIVERY.

Letters delivered	698,965	
Postal cards delivered	107,609	
Newspapers, packages, etc	244,800	
		1,051,374

MAILING DEPARTMENT.

Letters mailed and in transit	2,005,020	
Postal cards "	358,146	
2d, 3d and 4th class matter	1,477,975	
		3,901,141

GENERAL BUSINESS.

Total receipts from postage account	$30,645 91	
Balance on hand money order account January 1, 1889	251 59	
Total receipts for money orders and fees	55,706 02	
Transferred from postage to money order account	587 00	
		$87,190 52

Total expenses post office	$16,774 59	
Net income to department postage account	13,871 32	
Total money orders paid, etc.	47,856 84	
" cash remitted by draft money order account	8,485 00	
Balance on hand money order account December 31, 1889	202 77	
		$87,190 52

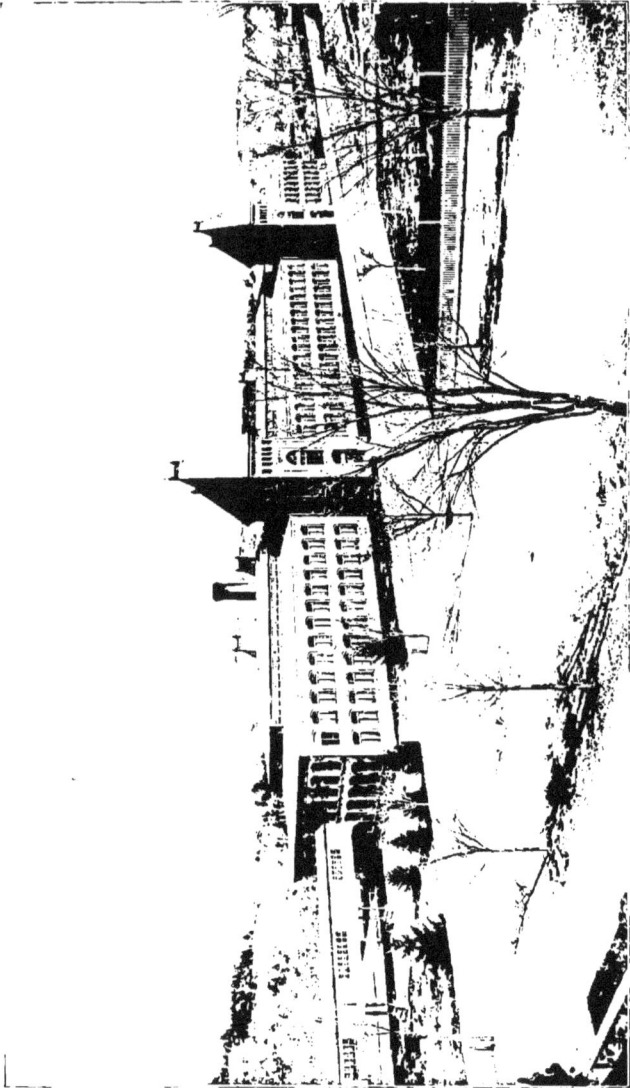

ANNEX PONEMAH MILLS, (TAFTVILLE), NORWICH, CONN.

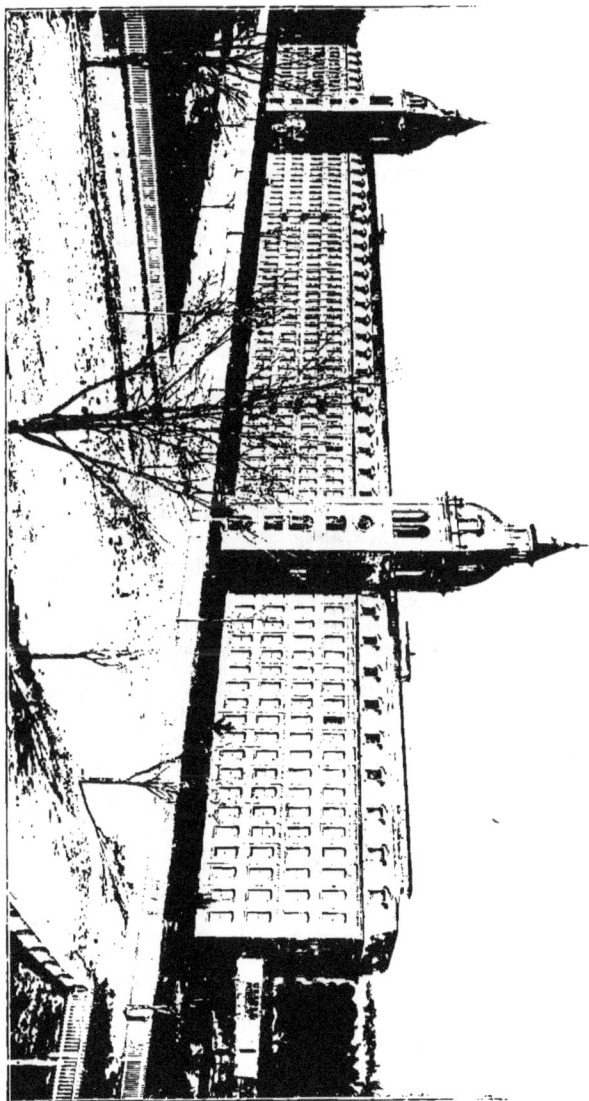

PONEMAH MILLS, (TAFTVILLE), NORWICH, CONN.

NORWICH BOARD OF TRADE.

1890.

OFFICERS.

President.—Henry H. Gallup.
Vice-Presidents. — Adams P. Carroll, Dr. P. Cassidy, Arthur H. Brewer.
Recording Secretary.—David R. Jones.
Corresponding Secretary.—Frank L. Woodard.
Treasurer—Jonathan Trumbull.
Executive Committee.—Henry H. Gallup, Adams P. Carroll, Arthur H. Brewer, Hugh H. Osgood, Wm. N. Blackstone, Dr. P. Cassidy, Edwin S. Ely, Solomon Lucas, Laban R. Jewett.
Committee on Trades and Manufactures.—A. H. Brewer, M. A. Barber, Chas. R. Butts, J. E. Warner, E. E. Page.

Committee on Entertainments.—J. DeT. Blackstone, H. E. Fisher, Z. R. Robbins, Geo. W. Carroll, Wm. C. Mowry.
Committee on Arbitration.—F. J. Leavens, J. F. Williams, Chas. B. Lee, Reuben S. Bartlett, W. A. Briscoe.
Committee on Transportation.—Dr. P. Cassidy, M. M. Whittemore, Arch. Mitchell, Adam Reid, Geo. C. Raymond.
Committee on Statistics.—Chas. E. Chandler, F. L. Woodard, F. H. Pullen, J. H. Keep, J. J. Desmond.

MEMBERS.

A. R. Aborn, William P. Adams, William A. Aiken, A. H. Almy, P. St. M. Andrews, J. H. Arnold, John C. Averill, O. P. Avery, N. E. Alling, Asa Backus, M. Angelo Barber, Charles Bard, John P. Barstow, R. S. Bartlett, A. A. Beckwith, Charles H. Beebe, Henry Bill, N. A. Bingham, C. C. Bliss, A. R. Birchard, B. P. Bishop, Herbert M. Bishop, N. L. Bishop, S. B. Bishop, J. De T. Blackstone, William N. Blackstone, S. E. Bliven, Junius A. Brand, Arthur H. Brewer, J. M. Brewer, E. M. Brewster, Willis A. Briscoe, Charles D. Browning, James A. Brown, John T. Brown, Robert Brown, Charles R. Butts, H. L. Butts, Frederick S. Camp, W. H. Cardwell, A. E. Carey, Increase W. Carpenter, Adams P. Carroll, George W. Carroll, L. W. Carroll, Patrick Cassidy, Chas. E. Chandler, Enoch F. Chapman, Allan Cleworth, Charles P. Cogswell, George D. Coit, P. R. Condon, A. T. Converse, Charles A. Converse, James F. Cosgrove, S. A. Crandall, B. T. Cranston, J. H. Cranston, C. H. Davis, George A. Davis, James Dawson, Jr., Norman Day, J. J. Desmond, F. E. Dowe, James Duggan, Charles E. Dyer, Charles S. Eaton, Luther S. Eaton, Edwin S. Ely, William G. Ely, H. E. Fisher, Oliver T. Forbes, John H. Ford, Geo. E. Fellows, H. H. Gallup, A. T. Gardner, Edward N. Gibbs, Joseph W. Gilbert, S. Alpheus Gilbert, George W. Gould, Gardiner Greene, Jr., C. R. Harrington, A. H. Harris, E. D. Harris, Luke M. Heery, G. L. Hewitt, Heyman J. Hirsch, Joseph Holmes, Roscoe Huntington, L. R. Jewett, Charles S. Johnson, Oliver L. Johnson, Jr., David R. Jones, Charles J. King, A. B. Kingsbury, John H. Keep, John H. Kelley, Geo. A. Lane, W. T. Lane, Arthur D. Lathrop, Bela P. Learned, Frank J. Leavens, Charles B. Lee, D. M. Lester, Solomon Lucas, R. W. Marshall, C. Michael McNamara, John McWilliams, A. G. Mitchell, Archibald Mitchell, Frank A. Mitchell, William C. Mowry, John P. Murphy, Charles D. Noyes, William M. Olcott, Charles H. Osgood, Fred L. Osgood, Hugh H. Osgood, A. T. Otis, Elmer E. Page, William H. Page, George S. Palmer, H. F. Palmer, William B. Parker, Seth L. Peck, John T. Perkins, Robert W. Perkins, Charles H. Phelps, John Porteous, A. L. Potter, George H. Pratt, Amos W. Prentice, Charles H. Preston, Frank H. Pullen, H. D. Rallion, George C. Raymond, Adam Reid, Z. R. Robbins, A. Irving Royce, Thomas D. Sayles, J. B. Shannon, William H. Shields, Rufus Sibley, Nathan Small, A. D. Smith, Frank H. Smith, George S. Smith, J. Hunt Smith, J. Palmer Story, Nicholas Tarrant, Archibald Troland, Jonathan Trumbull, William C. Tucker, F. C. Turner, Sidney Turner, Fred C. Tyler, Frank Ulmer, W. M. Vars, A. N. H. Vaughn, J. E. Warner, F. R. Wasley, David A. Wells, M. M. Whittemore, Jerome F. Williams, Winslow T. Williams, Chas. J. Winters, F. L. Woodard, F. H. Woodworth, Thomas B. Woodworth, E. B. Worthington.

OTIS LIBRARY, CORNER CHURCH AND BROADWAY.

The Library was establi...ed in 1849 by the late Joseph Otis, an expense of about $10,000, of wh. $6,000 was for the lot and building, and $4,000 for books. In addition to this, Mr. Otis, at his death, bequeathed a fund of $7,000 (which remains intact) the income of which was to be devoted to the purchase of books. A very liberal charter was granted by the State, and the management of the Library vested in a self-perpetuating board of seven trustees. The funds were added to, later, by the donation of $1,000 by Mr. Chas. Boswell, of West Hartford, a native of Norwich. Other friends have, from time to time, given valuable aid in money, and volumes from their private collections. The library contains over 16,000 well selected volumes. It also subscribes for more than forty leading American and foreign magazines and reviews. Many duplicates of popular books and magazines are bought, and these can afterwards be purchased at the very lowest rates. Catalogues can be consulted at the Library, especially the card catalogue, which is continually receiving new cards as new additions are made to the volumes on the shelves. Fresh additions, of best recent fiction, and of good books for children, are always to be had. The trustees intend to purchase all new works of popular interest as they appear, (avoiding, however, novels and juveniles which are bad in their moral teaching); and are also continually adding standard works of permanent value in the various departments of literature, science and art. The Library should contain every memorial, whether book, pamphlet, map, broadside, print, photograph, or the like, which is procurable, and which in any way illustrates the history or topography of Norwich ; and it is hoped that the friends of the Library will assist in making the collection complete.

For full privileges of the Library, including two books and a periodical at a time, the annual charge is $3. For two, books without periodicals, $2 ; one book alone, $1 ; periodicals, only $1. Books and periodicals are also let at two cents a day, or ten cents a week. The most popular new books can be kept seven days ; all others fourteen days, with privilege to renew. The librarian, upon request, will reserve any book one day, and give notice by postal card when it comes in. Books will also be delivered, or called for, in any part of the city at a small charge. Any desirable book not in the Library will be purchased at the request of the subscriber, if the funds of the Library will admit.

The Library is open daily (Sundays excepted) from 10 A. M. to 8 P. M.; on Saturday till 9 P. M.; Tuesdays and Thursdays close at 6 P. M. This is double the number of hours per week which the Library had previously been open, the trustees having made this new departure in the hope that the public will appreciate their opportunity, and, through greater use of the institution, more than make good the large additional expense involved. The subscribers should be increased from about four hundred, as at present, to three times that number.

The Library has recently been furnished with a card catalogue made in accordance with the plan adopted by many of the first libraries in the country.

Within the past two years it has begun to receive income from the munificent bequest of nearly thirteen thousand dollars by the late Dr. Daniel T. Coit.

Trustees : Wm. A. Aiken, Wm. S. Palmer, Jonathan Trumbull, E. N. Gibbs, Wm. A. Slater, F. T. Sayles.

President, Wm. A. Aiken ; Secretary, W. A. Briscoe ; Treasurer, Jonathan Trumbull ; Libra... Mrs. F. W. Robinson ; Assistant, Miss Juliet W. Robinson.

NORWICH SOLDIERS' MONUMENT.

During the summer months there is considerable interest manifested in boating. The Che   a Boat Club owns a fine house near the Main street bridge and its members may be seen any pleasa evening skimming over the Thames. Numerous other boats are owned in this vicinity and the beautiful coves about the river are frequent resorts for pleasure parties. While not a local affair, much interest is manifested in Norwich over the great aquatic contests which occur on the Thames every year between the great colleges, Harvard, Yale, Columbia, Cornell and University of Pennsylvania. These struggles have taken place every year without intermission since 1878, when the aquatic Titans, Yale and Harvard, made their first essay on the Thames as a rowing stream, and its great superiority to the Springfield lake, where they had been held formerly, was so obvious that this place has since been chosen without change. The final battles on

IRON'S COVE

HORTON'S COVE

the river come off during the last of June or first of July of each year, but for a month before that time the shadows of the coming events are cast largely before. Harvard, Yale, Columbia, Pennsylvania and Cornell owning boat houses on the Thames. During the week before the races the town is enlivened by the frequent coming and going of college men, anxious for a glance at their own pet champions; but the great interest and excitement culminates on the days of the races. The order of races is usually, the Yale-Pennsylvania freshman race, the Harvard-Columbia freshman race, the Yale-Pennsylvania University race, the Columbia-Cornell University race, and finally on the last great day the Harvard-Yale University race. On the latter day particularly the river and shore are an object of wonderful beauty and delight. Early in the day the river begins to swarm with gaily-decked craft, both small and large. Yachts with great streamers of blue or crimson bunting and

THE OLD CHELSEA BOAT HOUSE.

sheets strung with national flags, decks lined with enthusiastic and exuberant partisans take up their place along the sides of the course, on the east part above the finish. All the large and small steamers, pleasure boats and tugs along this section of the shore get ready to take their crowded loads of passengers up the river to follow the racers down. Some time before the race boats come down from Norwich and up from New Haven packed with eager spectators, and when at length the two brawny crews pull out from their boat-houses and line up at the stake-boat, the river seems to be fairly alive with an immense concourse of excited watchers. The scenes on shore are none the less marked. Above the finish line, on Winthrop Neck, is an immense grand stand, crowded with onlookers. The shores for long distances are also lined, and the long observation train of twenty-five or thirty cars filled to the brim, flying great banks of red and blue, and sending forth stunning peals of "Rah! Rah! Rah! Yale," "R-a-h! R-a-h! R-a-h! Harvard," draws its winding length slowly up opposite the starting line. Now for a moment there is breathlessness, then the pistol flashes, the stern-lines from the two boats are dropped by their holders, and off neck and neck go the two great sweeping lines of oars, followed at a regulated distance on the river by a great and imposing line of steamboats and smaller craft, on the shore by the observation train which now sends forth the sharp staccato Yale shout, or the longer, deeper Harvard cry, as the partisans of either side fancy they see their own colors to the fore. So for four miles straight away dash the two crews, followed with unbending gaze by some twenty thousand eyes, and unwearying exclamations from some ten thousand throats. In little more than twenty minutes, that seem as many days to the crews with every muscle strained to its utmost, and hardly more seconds to the vast watching concourse, and either the blue or the crimson has crossed the line, while cannons thunder from neighboring yachts, and the great annual conflict on which were settled so many ardent hopes, and not a few treasured and anxious dollars, is decided. The victors generally turn about on their oars, and row quietly and slowly back up the river, while the vanquished crew pant, stretched out at full length for a time, and then are towed back to their headquarters by their launch. The great crowd now begins to disperse, the air being rent with the shouts in which only one college name is heard, the others maintaining an unbroken silence.

The record of winners and times for the last twelve years since the races have been rowed on the Thames, will no doubt interest a good many :

RESIDENCE OF MR. GEO. S. SMITH.

JAS. A. HISCOX, Architect.

INDEX TO BUSINESS NOTICES.

32   INDEX TO BUSINESS NOTICES.

LEADING BUSINESS MEN OF NORWICH.

The Thames National Bank, Norwich, Ct.—Without attempting to estimate with any degree of precision the influence which the Thames National Bank has exerted in building up the mercantile and manufacturing interests of this section of the State, it may still be safely asserted that Norwich owes much to the enterprise and public spirit of those who have administered the affairs of the institution in question. The management of a representative city bank is by no means an easy task at the best, and during times of financial "panic" it calls for judgment and resolution of a high order, for the officials feel that much besides the continuance of their own enterprise depends upon the wisdom of their action, and appreciate the fact that a single false step may involve many important undertakings. It is perfectly safe to say that the business men of this section cordially endorse the Thames National Bank, and recognize the fact that it is conducted in the interest of the entire community and not of the stockholders alone, or indeed of any other class or faction. An institution conducted on so broad a basis with a capital of $1,000,000, and a surplus of half that amount, must of necessity have a much more than local reputation, and it is but simple justice to say that no bank in the entire State is more widely or favorably known. Organized as a State bank in 1824, it was incorporated under the national banking laws in 1865, and has since steadily progressed in influence and usefulness. No similar institution in New England is better prepared to transact a general banking business, and we may add that no bank carrying on operations on an equally large scale is more free from that excessive "red-tapeism" so distasteful to the average business man. The banking rooms are elegantly decorated and fitted up, being supplied with everything necessary to facilitate business to the highest degree. They are centrally located at No. 16 Shetucket street, in a commodious and handsome building of which the bank is owner. Mr. Franklin Nichols is president of the bank; Mr. Edward N. Gibbs being vice-president; Mr. Stephen B. Meech, cashier, and Mr. Charles W. Gale, assistant cashier; while the board of directors is composed of men largely and prominently identified with the representative business enterprises of Norwich and vicinity.

Directors: Franklin Nichols, Alfred A. Young, James L. Hubbard, Wm. G. Johnson, Hugh H. Osgood, John Mitchell, Thos. B. Sayles, Edw. N. Gibbs, Wm. A. Slater, Henry N. Gallup, Wm. N. Blackstone, Lucius Briggs.

Hislop, Porteous & Mitchell, wholesale and retail dealers in Dry and Fancy Goods, Carpets, Oilcloths, Upholstery Goods, etc. Strictly one price. Nos. 83, 93 and 95 Main Street; wholesale entrance 100–110 Water Street, Norwich, Conn.—Whatever may have been the case in the past, there is no denying that at the present time a business must either continually develop or decrease for there seems to be no such thing as standing still,—that is to say in such commercial centres as Norwich, New London, etc. A very prominent illustration of this fact is to be seen in the enterprise conducted by Messrs. Hislop, Porteous & Mitchell, at Nos. 93 and 95 Main street, and Nos. 100–110 Water street, for during the seventeen years that this undertaking has been carried on, its development has been both constant and rapid,—so rapid in fact as to have long since given the firm the reputation of being the leading house of the kind in the entire State. The modest establishment at No. 170 Main street, in which operations were begun in 1873, would not now accommodate a single one of the many important departments of the business, and in addition to the elegant and commodious establishment in this city, the firm maintain large branch stores at New London, and in New York State and Michigan. Mr. James Hislop is in charge of the New London store; Mr. Archibald Mitchell superintending the Norwich establishment, and Mr. John Porteous looking after the buying and other general interests of the firm. The Norwich store contains an immense stock of dry and fancy goods, carpetings, upholstery goods, etc., and by common consent is clearly entitled to the name of headquarters for these and kindred articles, for not only is the assortment the largest and the prices the lowest, but the goods are thoroughly dependable in every respect,—the fact that an article was bought from Messrs. Hislop, Porteous & Mitchell being accepted as convincing evidence that it will prove precisely as represented. A very large and efficient force of assistants is employed and despite the great magnitude of the business, callers are attended to with a promptness and courtesy that might be profitably imitated in many other establishments. This firm spare no pains to fully satisfy purchasers. That this policy is a popular one, is evident from the magnitude the business has attained, and the inducements offered are so genuine that we can give our readers no better advice than to give this establishment an early call.

Edward Chappell & Co., Coal and Lumber. Office, 46 to 76 West Main Street, Central Wharf; Branch Office, 213 Main Street, Franklin Square, Norwich, Conn.—It would be difficult to name another enterprise having so much dependent upon it as is the case with that conducted by Messrs. Edward Chappell & Co., for this representative firm deal very extensively in lumber and coal, and as they supply about all the large factories and other consumers in this vicinity with the latter commodity, a failure to satisfactorily meet the demands made upon them would have a powerful effect upon the manufacturing interests of this section. Happily there is not the slightest danger of any such failure, for the facilities under the control of this firm are unequalled, and in the future as in the past, will enable it to easily maintain the leading position and fill the most extensive orders at short notice. The premises made use of are located at Nos. 46 to 76 Main street, Central Wharf, and there is also a branch office maintained at No. 213 Main street, Franklin square. Some 20,000 tons of coal and 10,000,000 feet of lumber can be carried in stock at one time, and the arrangements for the reception, delivery and storage of the commodities dealt in must truly "be seen to be appreciated," for they are planned on too large a scale to render satisfactory description possible. About forty men are employed, and large and small orders are both assured immediate and painstaking attention, it being hardly necessary to add that the firm are prepared to quote bottom prices in every department of their business. Cargo lots supplied. This undertaking was founded in 1840 by Mr. Edward Chappell, who is a native of New London, but has been located in Norwich since 1837. He is heavily interested in various manufacturing enterprises and has done much to develop the resources of this vicinity. His associates in the present firm are Messrs. E. F. Chapman and A. H. Brewer, the former a native of New York City, and the latter of Norwich. Mr. Chapman has been connected with the firm since 1848 and has held various municipal offices, having served for years in the common council, etc. Mr. Brewer is as generally known in social as in business circles, and stands very high in Free Masonry, having taken all the degrees that can be granted in this country. He is one of the few men who can honestly be said to have "hosts of friends," for he is very popular throughout this section and is prominently identified with the Arcanum Club, and with other social organizations.

Cranston & Co. (formerly M. Safford & Co.), Jobbers and Retailers, Booksellers, Stationers and News Dealers, Artists' Materials and Photographic Supplies, 158 Main Street, Norwich, Conn —The enterprise carried on by Messrs. Cranston & Co., has practically completed its first half century of existence, for it was inaugurated in 1840 by Mr. M. Safford. The firm name of M. Safford & Co. was adopted in 1866, Mr. B. T. Cranston then becoming a partner, and in 1887 the present style was taken. As now constituted, the firm is made up Messrs. B. T., W. B. L. and T. H. Cranston, the first named being a native of Warren, R. I., while both his associates were born in Providence. The present store has been occupied for nearly a third of a century, but it is modern in style, having an attractive plate-glass front and being equipped with all necessary facilities. The premises comprise four floors of the dimensions of 40x20 feet, and contain a stock which it is safe to say cannot be paralleled in this city. The firm are jobbers and retailers of books, stationery, artists' materials, photographic supplies, etc., and make it a point to carry an assortment which will admit of all tastes and all purses being suited. The very lowest market rates are quoted on reliable goods. Photographers, both professional and amateur, would do well to visit this popular establishment, for only reliable supplies are dealt in and no pains is spared to assure satisfaction to every customer. There are five assistants employed, and callers may depend upon receiving prompt and polite attention.

J. F. Williams & Son, Fire and Marine Insurance Agency, Richards Building, 91 Main Street, Norwich, Conn.—The New London County Mutual Fire Insurance Company was organized in 1840 and during the past half-century has steadily maintained its position in the front ranks of mutual companies. It has paid for losses since July, 1840, a sum approximating $200,000, and the amount of risks now outstanding is not far from $4,000,000. This company is remarkable even among mutual companies for the lightness of its running expenses, and the character of the securities forming its assets shows very conservative and able management. The president is Mr. E. F. Parker, the secretary, Mr. J. F. Williams, and the board of directors is constituted of Messrs. E. F. Parker, John A. Morgan, P. S. M. Andrews, C. H. Osgood, John L. Boswell, J. F. Williams, C. J. Winters, F. L. Gardner, Ira L. Peck, F. L. Osgood and Charles P. Cogswell. The office of the company is in Richards Building, No. 91 Main street, where the secretary, Mr. Jerome F. Williams carries on a general insurance agency, being associated with Mr. L. H. Williams, under the firm name of J. F. Williams & Son. This is one of the most widely and favorably known agencies in the State, for it has been carried on for more than a quarter of a century and has an unblemished record for promptness and reliability Business was begun by the present senior partner in 1873, and Mr. L. H. Williams became associated with him in 1887. Both members of the firm are natives of Norwich, and Mr. J. F Williams is connected with the school board. Any amount of business may be placed through this firm on the most favorable terms, the following leading companies being represented: Sun Fire Office, London; Phœnix Insurance Co., London; West Chester, New York; Bowery, New York; Fire Association, London; Williamsburgh City Insurance Co., New York; Rochester German Insurance Co., Rochester; Buffalo German Insurance Co., Buffalo; Equitable Fire and Marine, Prov., R. I.; Providence-Washington, Prov., R. I.; Pacific, New York; Fireman's Fund, San Francisco; California, San Francisco; Commerce, Albany; New London County Mutual, Norwich; Lloyd's Plate Glass, New York.

F. P. Church & Co., manufacturers and dealers in Imported and Domestic Cigars, 72 Main Street, Norwich.—There is no firm doing business in this city which deserves more hearty and constant support from the smoking fraternity than does that of F. P. Church & Co., for this concern are manufacturers of and dealers in imported and domestic cigars, and spare no pains to offer goods that will prove precisely as represented and give the best of satisfaction to consumers. The healthfulness or unhealthfulness of smoking has caused almost endless discussion and given rise to many ingenious arguments on both sides of the question, but smokers and non smokers can consistently agree on one point—that if one is to smoke at all he should take care to use a pure and uniform grade of tobacco. Many a case of sickness has been ascribed to tobacco when if the truth were known it would not be the tobacco but the injurious flavoring or other adulterant used which should have been blamed. Carefully prepared tobacco, not artificially flavored, will injure no one if used in reasonable moderation, and those who assert the contrary take a position which experience does not maintain. Messrs. F. P. Church & Co carry a large assortment of foreign and domestic cigars in stock, and do both a wholesale and retail business, being prepared to fill the heaviest orders at short notice and to quote the lowest market rates. Their establishment is located at No. 72 Main street, and those in search of a good honest cigar at a good honest price will find just what they want at this popular store. A specialty is made of the manufacture of the popular ten cent cigar, "No. 10," of which many thousands have been sold. The present firm was formed in 1886, and is constituted of Messrs. F. P. Church and L. R. Church, both of whom are natives of Montville, and have a large circle of friends in this vicinity.

G. W. Hamilton, Fine Shoes, 134 Main Street, Norwich, Conn.—It is generally considered that the man who tries to suit everybody is very apt to find himself unable to suit anybody, but there are exceptions to all rules, and the experience of Mr. G. W. Hamilton would seem to indicate that intelligent efforts to please everybody will be appreciated by the public, for the gentleman in question has entered to all classes of trade since beginning operations in 1884, and has built up an extensive and desirable business. Mr. Hamilton deals in foot-wear of all descriptions and always carries a complete and carefully chosen stock of fine boots, shoes, rubbers, slippers, etc., which comprises the productions of the most reputable manufacturers and always includes the very latest fashionable novelties as well as full lines of staple goods. The premises occupied are located at No. 134 Main street, and are of the dimensions of 45 × 20 feet. The stock is displayed to excellent advantage and the store is well worthy of a visit, for goods are cheerfully shown, and three assistants are at hand to give prompt and courteous attention to callers. Mr. Hamilton is in a position to quote the very lowest market rates on all the goods he handles, and every article sold by him is guaranteed to prove precisely as represented in every respect.

J. Strauss & Co., dealers in Millinery, 124 Main Street, Norwich, Conn.—It is not at all surprising that the millinery business should have reached very large proportions in this city, for in addition to the extensive local trade there is a heavy out of town patronage, and this patronage is bound to continue to increase as it becomes more plainly evident that the leading Norwich millinery houses can successfully compete with those of New York in catering to non-resident patrons. The firm name of J. Strauss & Co. is very favorably known in connection with the handling of millinery, for this concern have done an extensive wholesale, retail and custom business for some years and have proved themselves to have facilities fully equal to the best. The premises utilized are located at No. 124 Main street, and have an area of about 1500 square feet, affording ample room for the carrying of a very heavy stock of millinery goods of every description. There is no really fashionable novelty in the millinery line but what may be obtained here as soon as it is placed upon the market, and the fact that the customers of J. Strauss & Co. include the most tasty and careful dressers, indicates that the policy of the firm in this respect is appreciated. The facilities for the doing of custom work are unsurpassed, twelve assistants being at hand to ensure the prompt and careful filling of every order.

L. W. Carroll & Son, Commission Merchants, Wool, Cotton, Manufacturers Supplies, Dye Stuffs, Paints, Oils, Glass, etc., etc., Nos. 17, 19 and 21 Water Street, Norwich, Conn.—Few men have been more active in developing the manufacturing and mercantile interests of Connecticut than has Mr. L. W. Carroll, of the well-known firm of L. W. Carroll & Son, and this gentleman's activity has been by no means confined to the business with which the firm in question is identified, for he has long been prominent in banking circles, was concerned in the origin of the Occum Water Power Company, and is proprietor of one of the best equipped cotton mills in the State. The enterprise carried on by Messrs. L. W. Carroll & Son, was inaugurated in 1843 by Messrs Carroll & Crosby, Mr. L. W. Carroll assuming sole control the following year and admitting Mr. A. P. Carroll to partnership under the existing firm name in 1876. A very extensive commission business is done, the concern dealing in wool, cotton, manufacturers' supplies, paints, oils, glass, dye stuffs, etc., and carrying an immense stock which necessitates the occupancy of one of the largest warehouses in the city, the premises in use comprising six floors of the dimensions of 35 × 110 feet. They are located at Nos. 17, 19 and 21 Water street, and eight assistants are at hand to give prompt and careful attention to every order.

Noyes & Davis, wholesale and retail Booksellers and Stationers; Headquarters for Blank Books, School Books and School Supplies of all kinds; Base Balls, Bats, Lawn Tennis and Croquet, 152 and 154 Main Street, Norwich, Conn.—One of the most truly popular establishments to be found in this city is that conducted by Messrs. Noyes & Davis, at Nos. 152 and 154 Main street, and one only needs to visit this store and to use his eyes and ears in order to obtain a satisfactory explanation of the high favor in which it is held by all classes of people. The premises are 45 × 35 feet in dimensions and contain a most skillfully chosen stock, made up of books, stationery, fancy goods, blank books, base ball supplies, lawn tennis and croquet goods, etc. During the vacation season a specialty is made of out-door games, etc., but at other times of year, particular attention is paid to the handling of school books and school supplies of all kinds, and with such success that this store is universally regarded as the headquarters for these goods. The very latest fashionable novelties in stationery are also obtainable here as soon as they appear in the market, and a full assortment of business stationery is always carried. The store has telephone connection, and orders thus received are assured as prompt and careful attention as those given in person. This business was founded about a quarter of a century ago by Mr. S. B. Bishop, and the present firm have been in charge since 1873. The partners are Messrs. C. D. Noyes and George A. Davis, both of whom are too well known in this vicinity to call for extended personal mention. They give close attention to the business and are excellently prepared to fill wholesale and retail orders without delay and at the lowest market rates.

Norwich Gas-Light Co., Norwich Electric-Light Co., 40 Shetucket Street, Norwich, Conn.—The Norwich Gas-Light Company and the Norwich Electric-Light Company are separate and distinct corporations, but they supplement one another so perfectly in the service offered to the public that it is fitting they should be mentioned together, especially as those prominent in one company are also interested in the other. Those who predicted that electricity would drive gas from the field as an illuminant were far too premature in their prophecy, for although it is probable that electricity will gradually supersede gas for lighting purposes, still the movement is bound to be slow and will work no hardship to those largely interested in gas company stock. On the other hand, gas is unquestionably the fuel of the future, and as a superior quality of heating gas can be manufactured at a much less expense than can illuminating gas, there is no danger but that the mains and other plant now in use will find profitable employment for an indefinite time in the future. The Norwich Gas-Light Company was incorporated in 1854, and has a capital of $125,000. It furnishes a very desirable quality of gas for illuminating purposes, and the prices quoted have always compared favorably with those named by other corporations doing business under similar conditions. The president is Mr. Franklin Nichols, the secretary and treasurer, Mr. C. C. Johnson, and the superintendent, Mr. O. Gilmore; the directors being constituted as follows: Franklin Nichols, C. C. Johnson, E. N. Gibbs, F. L. Osgood, W. A. Slater, John M. Johnson.

The Norwich Electric-Light Company was incorporated in 1881 and has gained the good-will of resident business men and others by its progressive and accommodating methods and by the reliability and cheapness of the service rendered. The company are prepared to supply 800 incandescent, and seventy-six arc lights, and operate four large dynamos; the capital invested being $25,000. New and extensive works on North Main street are in process of erection. The president is Mr. H. H. Osgood, the secretary and treasurer, Mr. C. C. Johnson, and the superintendent, Mr. George W. Phillips, while the board of directors is made up of Messrs. H. H. Osgood, E. N. Gibbs, J. Hunt Smith, William A. Slater and John M. Johnson. The offices of both the Gas-light and the Electric-light companies are at No. 40 Shetucket street.

H. R. Woodward, Diamonds, Watches, Jewelry, Silverware, and Optical Goods. Wholesale and Retail. Fine Watch and French Clock Repairing, Fine Engraving a Specialty. 163 Main Street, Norwich, Conn., Branch Store at Gardiner, Maine.— There are few if any enterprises of no longer establishment which have gained so high a place in the favor of the purchasing public as is held by that conducted by Mr. H. R. Woodward, at No. 163 Main street, and this popularity is all the more worthy of mention from the fact that it has been brought about by strictly legitimate methods and hence is sure to be lasting and progressive. Operations were begun here April, 1883, but Mr. Woodward has been in the wholesale line for the past twelve years and also conducts another store at Gardiner, Maine. Mr. Geo. S. Lathrop has for the past four years represented Mr. Woodward as travelling salesman. The store in Gardiner, Maine, which is the leading jewelry store in town, has been known as a jewelry store thirty-three years. Both stores are headquarters for diamonds, watches, jewelry, silverware and optical goods, for Mr. Woodward deals in all these articles, doing both a wholesale and retail business and offering inducements which argue very favorable relations with manufacturers and a disposition to be content with a very small margin of profit. The stock in both places is remarkably complete in its various departments and comprises a full selection of the latest fashionable novelties in the jewelry line, including some beautiful and tasteful designs for engagement rings. Silverware, both solid and plated, is extensively handled, and so are watches and parlor clocks, some very reliable timepieces being offered at low rates. Fine watch and French clock repairing is a prominent feature of the business, and a specialty is made of fine engraving, orders being executed at short notice in the highest style of the art. Mr. Woodward employs three efficient assistants at each store but gives careful personal attention to the supervision of affairs. He is very popular among his customers and has a large circle of friends. None of our local business men have worked harder to attain success, and Mr. Woodward has certainly been very successful.

C. T. & W. F. Bidwell, Boots, Shoes, Slippers, Rubbers. No. 138 Main Street, Norwich, Conn.—What may justly be regarded as the representative establishment of the kind in this city is that conducted by Messrs. C. T. & W. F. Bidwell, at No. 138 Main street. The enterprise carried on by this firm was inaugurated in 1843 by Mr. I. M. Bidwell, who continued the business in partnership with his son for some years and was finally succeeded by him, Mr. E. G. Bidwell remaining sole proprietor up to 1884, when the existing firm assumed control. Both partners are natives of Norwich and are connected with the Free Masons and the Odd Fellows , having a very extensive acquaintance in both business and social circles. The firm utilize two floors of the dimensions of 55 × 25 feet, the store being magnificently fitted-up, and indeed comparing favorably with the leading Metropolitan establishments of a similar character. The public, however, are more immediately interested in the stock carried than in the premises which contain it, and we only regret that lack of space forbids our describing it somewhat in detail for it is well worthy of such mention, being composed of the finer grades of foot wear and containing the very latest fashionable novelties in every department. Both a wholesale and retail business is done, but especial attention is given to the latter and a very extensive and desirable patronage is enjoyed. Messrs. C. T. & W. F. Bidwell are close and careful buyers and maintain such relations with leading manufacturers as enable the firm to quote exceptionally low rates. Employment is given to two experienced and polite assistants and callers are assured immediate and painstaking attention.

Lee & Osgood, wholesale and retail Druggists, dealers in Paints, Oils, Lamp Chimneys, Window Glass, Mineral Waters and popular Patent Medicines, 129, 131 and 133 Main Street, and 150, 152 and 154 Water Street, Norwich, Conn.—There are certain firm-names which have been so long and so prominently identified with the business interests of Norwich that one can hardly think of that city without these representative concerns being brought to mind, and among them no one is more generally and favorably known than that of Lee & Osgood, doing business at Nos. 129, 131 and 133 Main street, and Nos. 150, 152 and 154 Water street. This firm name was adopted over half a century ago, and although Mr. H. H. Osgood has long been sole proprietor the original style is still adhered to. Mr. Osgood has been mayor of this city and is too well known in business and social circles to render detailed personal mention at all necessary. The firm occupy very spacious premises, comprising five floors of the dimensions of 60 × 40 feet and three floors measuring 50 × 30 feet, and, as may well be imagined from the vast storage capacity utilized, they carry an immense stock, complete in every department and remarkably varied and comprehensive. It is made up of drugs, medicines and chemicals of every description; paints, oils and window glass, lamp chimneys, mineral waters, popular patent medicines and other articles far too numerous to mention. Both a wholesale and retail business is carried on, and the magnitude of the trade is indicated by the fact that employment is given to fifteen assistants. This large force enables the firm to fill all orders, large or small, at short notice, and the promptness of the service, the quality of the goods and the lowness of the prices fully justify and explain the general popularity of the establishment.

Smith & Gilbert, Merchant Tailors. Men's Furnishing Goods, Fine Shirts made to measure. 140 Main Street, Norwich, Conn.—There is a certain class which will always prefer custom made clothing, and there is another class which will be satisfied with ready made garments, so that there is no real danger of these two branches of trade interfering with one another. The well-informed public know that superior ready-made garments are preferable to inferior custom clothing, and they also know that the highest class of custom work is so far superior to the highest grade of ready-made work that no comparison is possible. Therefore it is obvious that one should either place his order with a first-class merchant tailoring firm or else purchase high-grade ready-made garments, and in our opinion the first course is the more economical as well as the more satisfactory in other respects. No better clothing is made in this State than that produced by Messrs. Smith & Gilbert, doing business at No. 140 Main street, and when its wearing qualities are duly considered and the moderate charges made are brought to mind, we believe that it will be found to be cheaper than presentable ready-made garments. The firm in question do a very extensive business, and utilize two floors of the dimensions of 60×30 feet. They carry a heavy, varied and seasonable stock of foreign and domestic fabrics, and men's furnishing goods and always present the latest fashionable novelties for their customers to choose from. Employment is given to thirteen competent assistants, and orders can be filled at short notice; it being understood, of course, that perfection of fit and thoroughness of workmanship are guaranteed. An important department of the business is the making of fine shirts to measure, and the most fastidious cannot help being satisfied with the results attained. This enterprise was started more than a quarter of a century ago by Messrs. Hayes & Smith, and the present firm was formed in 1875. Mr. A. D. Smith is a native of Worcester, Mass., and was formerly connected with the city council, while Mr. J. W. Gilbert was born in Stafford, Conn. Both these gentlemen give careful personal attention to the carrying on of the business and no trouble is spared to fully maintain the enviable reputation for promptness and reliability which has been held for so long a period.

J. McJennett, Hosiery, Gloves, Laces, Corsets, etc. Art Embroidery Materials. 144 Main Street, Norwich.—The store of which Mr. J. McJennett is the proprietor, located at No. 144 Main street, is one of those establishments which may be patronized again and again with ever increasing satisfaction, for the reliability of the goods, the lowness of the prices and the promptness and courtesy of the service, all combine to make this a favorite with discriminating purchasers. The proprietor is a native of Scotland, and established his present enterprise about 1877. He is exceptionally familiar with the many details of his business, and being a close and skillful buyer, is enabled to offer many marked inducements to his patrons. The stock on hand is so large and varied that we can do but little more than mention the more important articles it comprises, such as hosiery, gloves, laces, embroideries, ribbons, buttons, small wares and fancy goods, a specialty of art embroidery materials, and particular attention is given to the handling of corsets, ladies' white underwear, children's short and long cambric dresses, capes and lace caps. Mr. McJennett makes it a rule to offer his customers the very latest fashionable novelties to choose from, and to quote prices that will bear the very closest examination and comparison. He employs two efficient assistants, and every caller is sure of receiving prompt, careful and polite attention.

N. E. Alling, wholesale and retail dealer in Rubber Goods of every description, 11 Main Street and 22 Water Street, Norwich, Conn.—With the exception of iron, and of paper, and of wood, there is no material so generally useful as rubber, and considering the almost endless successful applications which have been made of it during the comparatively few years it has been upon the market, no reasonable limit can be set to its wider usefulness in the future. An immense amount of capital is invested in the production of rubber goods, and as each of the many concerns in the business has certain specialties in which it excels, it is obvious that the most convenient as well as the surest way to "get the best" is to buy, not of the agents of any particular company or firm, but of a dealer who handles the productions of all reputable rubber manufacturers. Such a dealer is Mr. N. E. Alling, and as he sells both at wholesale and retail he is prepared to furnish rubber goods of every description, in quantities to suit and at the lowest market rates. Mr. Alling carries a very heavy and varied stock, utilizing the spacious premises at No. 11 Main street, and No. 22 Water street, and sparing no pains to keep his assortment as complete as possible in every department. It is very generally understood that it is practically impossible in the majority of instances for the ordinary purchaser to distinguish between the good and the bad in rubber goods by superficial examination, and as their quality is apt to vary greatly with different manufacturers, the advantage of buying from a responsible dealer who guarantees his articles to prove as represented is obvious. •

Dodge & Holloway, Clothing and Gent's Furnishing Goods, No. 132 Main Street, Norwich, Conn.—The establishment conducted by Messrs. Dodge & Holloway, at No. 132 Main street, is a very old stand indeed, and was occupied by Mr. Pliny Brewer for more than forty years before he was succeeded by the present concern in 1889, but were its age its only recommendation we would not take up the time of our readers in writing about it, for this book has to do with the live concerns of to-day and not with the relics of a bye gone period. But Messrs. Dodge & Holloway do not depend upon the past to distinguish their establishment, on the contrary they are fully alive to the demands of the present day and offer inducements to purchasers of clothing, gentlemen's furnishings, etc., which are by no means easy to parallel elsewhere. The store is almost sixty feet deep, and contains a stock which must truly be seen to be appreciated, for it includes nothing but fresh, seasonable and fashionable goods, selected expressly for city trade and sure to give satisfaction to the most critical. The prices, too, are "right" in every respect, and not the least commendable feature of the management is the prompt and polite attention assured to every caller. Mr. Frank I. Dodge is a native of Norwich and has a very large circle of friends in this city, while Mr. George A. Holloway was born in Groton, and is also widely and favorably known in business and social circles.

The People's Industrial Insurance Co. Paid up Capital, $100,000; Authorized Capital, $500,000. 15 Main Street, Norwich, Conn.—Were all corporations conducted on the same general principles which have characterized the management of the People's Industrial Insurance Company since its organization, there would not be that widespread jealousy and mistrust of corporate enterprises now so evident among the people, for the company in question has steadily and rapidly gained in popularity from year to year and has repeatedly proved itself to be worthy of every confidence. It created a favorable impression at the outset of its career by beginning operations as a strictly *independent* company; not bound by the rules of any trust and therefore free to carry out whatever contracts might be made; and this independence has been steadily maintained up to the present time. Being, as its name indicates, a "People's" company, it seeks to avoid all unnecessary red tape and unessential formalities, the result being that one is not obliged to be a lawyer in order to understand the contracts, while policy holders may safely depend upon having claims paid *immediately* on completion of proofs of loss at the home office. Industrial insurance meets the wants of the people and thousands insure in the People's Industrial who would never think of taking out policies in ordinary insurance companies, for under the plan followed by the People's Company the cost of insurance is from five cents per week upwards and no increase of payments is required. Dues are collected weekly at the houses of the policy holders, thus obviating all trouble and loss of time. Five cents per week is so small a sum that no family would miss it, and yet it will insure a child aged from one to thirteen years, for various amounts up to $120. Ten cents per week will insure a person aged twenty for $202. Twenty five cents per week will insure a person aged thirty for $390. Fifty-five cents per week will insure a person aged twenty-one for $1,078. This being the case, who will say that small sums of money cannot be profitably invested ? Another point worthy of mention is that this company affords "insurance that insures." The directors are men who are very widely and favorably known in the community and who would never lend their names to any enterprise not carried on in accordance with sound and honorable business principles. The company has a paid up capital of $100,000, and authorized capital of half a million, and is easily able to meet all demands made upon it. The home office is located in this city, in Carroll Block, No. 15 Main street, and callers will cheerfully be given any information desired. The following list of officers and directors will show the kind of men identified with this popular and deserving undertaking:

President : Hugh H. Osgood.
Vice President, Wm. Fairbanks.
Second Vice President and Treasurer, Andrew E. Carey.
Secretary, Sherman B. Bishop.
Counsellor, Jeremiah Halsey.
Actuary, Levi W. Meech.
Medical Examiner, William Witter, M. D.
Board of directors, Hugh H. Osgood, Ex-Mayor of Norwich; Sherman B. Bishop, Secretary; Andrew E. Carey, Second Vice-President and Treasurer; William Fairbanks, Vice President; A. L. Williston, President First National Bank, Northampton, Mass.; S. Henry Whitcomb, President Whitcomb Envelope Co., Worcester, Mass.; John E. Warner, Secretary Hopkins & Allen Mfg. Company; Henry H. Gallup (Gallup & Ulmer), Norwich Belt Mfg. Co.; J. Palmer Story, General Insurance Agent.
Norwich agents, Butler Bros. and A. A. Hayward.

B. A. Herrick, Wauregan House Pharmacy, Norwich, Conn.—The Wauregan House Pharmacy is doubtless pleasantly familiar to many of our readers, for it has for some years ranked very high among local retail drug stores and is to-day unquestionably as well managed an establishment of the kind as can be found in this State. The patrons of a pharmacy have a right to expect the utmost caution on the part of the management when they are called upon to compound physicians' prescriptions, and we are happy to say that this expectation is fully realized in the case of the establishment in question, for the proprietor, Mr. B. A. Herrick, spares no pains to guard against the possibility of even the slightest error, and has provided the most elaborate and improved facilities for the measuring and general handling of the drugs and chemicals dealt in. The preparation of physicians' prescriptions is recognized as the most important feature of the business, and the many orders daily filled show that the public are appreciative of the advantages here offered. Mr. Herrick is a native of this State and has conducted his present enterprise since 1883. He gives close personal attention to the supervision of affairs, and employs three competent and polite assistants, so that despite the magnitude of the business, every caller is sure of receiving immediate and careful attention. The stock includes not only drugs, medicines and chemicals of every description, but also toilet and fancy articles, etc., the latest novelties being represented and moderate charges being made in connection with all the various articles handled.

T. J. Falvey, Hats, Caps and Gents' Furnishings, 74 Main Street, opposite Post Office, Norwich, Conn.—It would, of course, be a most excellent thing if all of us had so large an income as to render it entirely unnecessary to practice the close economy which is now the rule rather than the exception, but as this desirable condition of affairs is out of the question, the next best thing is to manage so as to make our present income go as far as possible. So far as the purchase of hats, caps and gents' furnishings is concerned this can be brought about by placing orders with Mr. T. J. Falvey, doing business at No. 74 Main street, opposite the Post Office, for Mr. Falvey carries a large and varied stock of such goods and quotes the very lowest market rates on them at all times. He is a native of Lebanon, Conn., and has been identified with his present establishment since 1885. The premises in use have an area of 1000 square feet, and afford ample opportunity for the display of the heavy stock to excellent advantage, making the task of selection both easy and agreeable. Mr. Falvey makes it a point to offer his customers the very latest fashionable novelties to choose from, and those who wish to dress in accordance with the very latest dictates of fashion and yet do not care to pay exorbitant prices can possibly find no more advantageous establishment at which to deal.

Edward D. Fuller & Co., dealers in Groceries, Provisions, Flour, Wooden Ware, Foreign and Domestic Fruits, Butter, Cheese, etc., etc., Nos. 45, 47, 49 and 51 Water Street, Norwich, Conn.—The liberal space we have given in this book to notices of the representative retail grocery houses of Norwich and vicinity, shows how we appreciate the importance of this branch of trade and gives amply sufficient reason why we should make mention of such an establishment as that conducted by Messrs. Edward D. Fuller & Co., for our retail grocers are of course directly dependent upon local wholesale houses for the nature of the service they are prepared to offer, and the concern in question ranks with the leading wholesale grocery and provision dealers of the State. The business was founded more than sixty years ago, operations having been begun by Messrs. Backus & Norton, in 1827. The firm of Case & Fuller assumed control in 1878, and the present style was adopted in December, 1888. An immense stock is carried, as indeed may be judged from the size of the premises occupied, these being numbered 45, 47, 49 and 51 Water street, and being fitted up with all necessary facilities for the handling and the storage of goods ; which latter fact has much to do with the reputation the firm enjoys for filling all orders at short notice and with perfect accuracy. Among the more prominent commodities handled may be mentioned staple and fancy groceries, provisions, flour, wooden ware, foreign and domestic fruits, butter, cheese and country produce in general ; and we may add that no concern is better prepared to supply canned goods, put up by the most reputable packers, in quantities to suit and at positively bottom prices. The store has telephone connection and five assistants are at hand to ensure the prompt and satisfactory filling of orders.

Second National Bank, Norwich, Conn.—First-class banking facilities may not produce business, but they certainly tend to develop it largely, and there is no question but that, other things being equal, the community having the best banking facilities will gain the most prosperity and prominence. It would, of course, be absurd to maintain that our local manufacturers and local commerce have reached their present development solely through the operations of the various banks here located, but it would be equally absurd to deny that these institutions have exerted a very appreciable influence in stimulating the industrial and mercantile growth of the city. The Second National Bank may fairly be taken as a representative Norwich financial institution for it has been carried on for a full quarter of a century, and stands to-day high in the confidence of the general public. This bank was incorporated in 1864, with a capital of $300,000, and it has established such favorable relations with correspondents throughout the country as to be in a position to offer unsurpassed advantages to patrons as regards the promptness, accuracy and zeal with which all business entrusted to it is transacted. The bank has a very large surplus, and its financial condition could hardly be improved upon, while the experience and standing of the officers and directors form the best possible evidence that, in the future as in the past, the credit of the institution will steadily be preserved above suspicion. The capital is $300,000 and surplus $60,000. The following list of those concerned in its management is made up of the names of business men thoroughly identified with Norwich and her interests, and prominent in manufacturing as well as in financial circles :

President, E. R. Thompson.
Vice President, C. P. Cogswell.
Cashier, Ira L. Peck.
Directors, E. R. Thompson, C. P. Cogswell, W. R. Burnham, W. R. Austin, Lyman Gould.

Alfred Hough, Specialties in Dress Trimmings, Laces and Fancy Goods. Orders will receive prompt and personal attention; 13 Main Street, Carroll Building, opposite Breed Hall, Norwich, Conn.—The phrase "a long-felt want," has been used so often and worn so threadbare that it deserves honorable retirement from active service, but it is so compactly descriptive a term that it can hardly be spared and we must utilize it once more in referring to the enterprise conducted by Mr. Alfred Hough, 13 Main street (Carroll Building, opposite Breed Hall), for this undertaking most certainly has supplied a "long-felt want," as is evidenced by the cordial support given to it since its inception in March, 1889. Mr. Hough handles specialties in dress trimmings, laces and fancy goods, and his stock is worthy the careful inspection of every lady in the city, for it is remarkably complete and desirable, and comprises not a few articles which it would be difficult if not impossible to find elsewhere in this vicinity. The premises occupied are 35 × 45 feet in dimensions, and the stock on hand is displayed to excellent advantage, being tastefully and conveniently arranged so that examination is easy and pleasant. Mr. Hough makes a practice of giving prompt personal attention to orders for goods not in stock, matching trimmings, ribbons, etc., etc., and with the aid of two assistants is prepared to assure immediate and courteous service to all who may favor his establishment with a call.

Henry Allen & Son, Undertakers; Residences, 92 and 94 Main, and 40 Church Streets. Office 98 Main Street, Norwich, Conn.—The enterprise conducted by Messrs. Henry Allen & Son, at No. 98 Main street, up-stairs, is most certainly deserving of prominent and favorable mention among the leading and typical undertakings of this section, for it was inaugurated more than a quarter of a century ago and for many years has held its present leading position. Operations were begun by Mr. Henry Allen in 1862, and in 1871 the existing firm-name was adopted, Mr. Amos D. Allen being admitted to partnership. Eleven years later Mr. William H. Allen became a member of the firm which now consists of Messrs. Henry, Amos and William Allen, the first-named being a native of Windham, while both his sons were born in this city. The premises utilized comprise three buildings, one of which contains one floor, measuring 70 × 40 feet, the other two having three floors of the dimensions of 80 × 35 feet. The firm have four fine hearses, one costing $1,500, being the finest in Eastern Connecticut. All the newest and best improved methods have been added to the equipment of the establishment and the finest undertaking work is executed. They are located at No. 98 Main street, nearly opposite the Western Union Telegraph Company's office, and as the residence of the members of the firm is at the west end of the same premises, orders may be left at all hours with the certainty of their receiving immediate and careful attention. Employment is given to three competent assistants, and as for the facilities at hand it is only necessary to say that they are amply sufficient to fully maintain the old-established reputation of this concern for promptness and thoroughness. The stock comprises coffins, caskets, robes and funeral goods of every description, these articles being handled both at wholesale and retail, and being furnished at the lowest market rates at all times. The entire charge of funerals will be assumed when desired, and entirely satisfactory service will be rendered at uniformly low rates.

Geo. W. Kies & Co., wholesale and retail dealers in Boots, Shoes and Rubbers, 80 Main Street (directly opposite the Post Office), Norwich, Conn.—A man who has carried on a certain line of business for more than a score of years should certainly be thoroughly conversant with it in every detail and should therefore be in a position to offer unsurpassed inducements to his customers, and we are sure that no one familiar with the facts will dispute that such is the case with George W. Kies & Co., doing business at No. 80 Main street. This enterprise was inaugurated by Mr. Kies in 1860, and the present firm was

formed in 1883 by the admission of Mr. James L. Coffee, who had been connected with the business in the capacity of salesman for thirteen years previous to that date. The senior partner is a native of Danielsonville, and his associate was born in this city. The premises now occupied are located directly opposite the post office, and as they have an area of about 1500 square feet, are capable of accommodating a large and varied stock. Considering the long experience of both the proprietors it becomes almost unnecessary to state that this stock is composed exclusively of reliable and desirable goods, and that the prices quoted are as low as can be named on dependable footwear. The latest fashionable novelties are at hand to choose from, and a large force of competent assistants assures immediate and polite attention to every caller.

C. J. King, dealer in Flour, Grain, Meal, Feed, Baled Hay, etc., No. 41 Commerce Street, Norwich, Conn.—There are many reasons why the enterprise conducted by Mr. C. J. King, at No. 41 Commerce street, should be regarded as a truly representative one, for during the more than sixty years that it has been carried on it has been honorably and intelligently managed, and is to-day without doubt as generally popular an undertaking of the kind as can be found in this city. Operations were begun about the year 1829, and the present proprietor has had control for nearly a score of years, he assuming possession in 1871. Mr. King is a native of Greene county, N. Y., and is one of the best-known of our resident merchants, both in trade and in social circles. He has very appreciably developed his business in every department, and gives it that close and careful personal attention which is indispensable to the attainment of the best results. Four floors are made use of, each of which measures 35 × 60 feet, and this large amount of space is all required in order to properly accommodate the very heavy stock, which comprises flour, grain, meal, feed, baled hay, etc., and is always complete in every department. Mr. King does both a wholesale and retail business and offers unsurpassed inducements to both classes of buyers. He employs about nine assistants on the average, and is always prepared to meet all demands upon him, his facilities for filling orders at short notice being all that could be desired.

John F. Parker, Insurance Agency, Room No. 3, Chelsea Savings Bank Building, Shetucket Street, Norwich, Conn.—The insurance agency conducted by Mr. John F. Parker, in room No. 3, Chelsea Savings Bank building, Shetucket street, was founded just about a quarter of a century ago, operations having been begun in 1865 by Mr. Thomas H. Perkins. The mere fact that this agency has received public support for so extended a period is of itself enough to establish its representative position, without taking into account the prominence due to the magnitude of the operations carried on. Mr. Parker represents fire and life companies having aggregate assets of over $30,000,-000, and among these organizations are numbered some of the very strongest insurance companies in the world; leading English as well as representative American corporations being acted for. As might reasonably be judged, in view of Mr. Parker's long and varied experience in his present line of business, he is in a position to offer inducements second to none in the line of strictly equitable insurance at strictly equitable rates. Callers are always assured immediate and courteous attention, and an idea of the character and scope of the business may be gained from the following list of companies represented :
Hartford, Hartford; Connecticut, Hartford; Orient, Hartford; North British and Mercantile, England; Queen, England; Imperial, England; Northern, England; Fire Association, Philadelphia; American, Philadelphia; Albany, Albany, N. Y.; Trans-Atlantic, Hamburg, Germany; Middlesex Mutual, Middletown; New London County Mutual, Norwich; Travelers' (Life and Accident), Hartford. Aggregate Assets, $30,000,000.

Elias H. Chapman, dealer in Boots, Shoes, etc., 104 Main Street, Norwich, Conn.—There is no single article of dress which the average person exercises more care in choosing than that of foot-wear, and there is excellent reason for this, for not only one's personal appearance but one's comfort also is largely dependent upon the boots or shoes worn. Those who have made a study of the matter assert that no two individuals' feet are exactly alike, there being certain peculiarities of shape in every instance, the same as there are certain peculiarities of feature which render every individual distinguishable from his fellows ; and as this is the case it is evident that the only way to properly cater to all tastes and all requirements is to carry so large a stock that the most varying demands can be satisfied. In this connection we may properly call attention to the assortment offered by Mr. E. H. Chapman at No. 104 Main Street, for this is complete in every department and is composed of the productions of the best-equipped and most popular manufacturers. Mr. Chapman is a native of Griswold and founded his present business in 1888. He at present is Treasurer and Clerk of the town of Griswold, and is very generally and favorably known throughout this vicinity. The premises utilized comprise two floors of the dimensions of 35 × 20 feet, and the stock is displayed to excellent advantage, making the task of selection an easy and agreeable one. Employment is afforded to two efficient assistants and prompt and courteous attention is assured to all, bottom prices being quoted on all the goods dealt in. Mr. Chapman has also been a partner for the past thirteen years of the firm of Potter & Chapman, of Jewett City.

The Gates Photo Studio, Miss E. M. Gates, Proprietress; W. D. Hickmott, Operator; 161 Main Street, Norwich, Conn.—Wonderful progress has been made in photography of late years, but the taste of the public has advanced as rapidly as has the art itself and consequently only the very best of work is now in request among the most desirable class of patrons. This is as it should be, for such a condition of affairs stimulates operators to do their best and assures continued and rapid progress. It is because we know that no better work is turned out in this city that we take especial pleasure in calling attention to "The Gates Photographic Studio," at No. 161 Main street, for this studio is equipped with the latest improved apparatus, is in charge of an experienced and skillful operator, and is well worthy of the generous patronage it has thus far received. These premises have been utilized for photographic purposes for many years but only came into the possession of Miss E. M. Gates, the present proprietress, in April, 1889. Miss Gates refitted the studio throughout, sparing no expense and neglecting no precaution that would tend to ensure more uniformity of excellence in the results attained. Under the present management first class work only is done; all work being guaranteed satisfactory in every respect. The prices are as low as is consistent with the carrying out of such a policy; being $5.00 per dozen for cabinets, and $2.50 per dozen for cards. A specialty is made of large work, and elegant life size portraits may be obtained here at moderate rates. The operator, Mr. W. D Hickmott, has had long and varied experience, and the best voucher of his skill is that afforded by the work on exhibition at the studio. Mr. Hickmott is just as anxious as his customers to attain the best results, and offers the following suggestions to intending sitters. They are the outcome of practical experience and are worthy of being strictly followed:

The best dress materials, and those which give the richest effects are silks, satins, reps, cashmeres and brocades. The most suitable colors are black, the different shades of green, brown, gray or slate for elderly people. For children, light colored costumes are the most suitable. Avoid dressing the hair in an unusual style. The operator can best determine the most graceful pose; and having his own reputation at stake, all may safely be left to his care. Cloudy weather is just as suitable.

The Wm. H. Page Wood Type Co., New Patented Process Type, 286-296 Franklin Street, Norwich, Conn.—The perfection of wood type has been a great boon to printers and has aided so materially in the attainment of the highest possibilities of job printing that there is not an office in the country, making any pretensions to a place in the front rank, which does not make some use of wood type. This line of manufacture was in a very crude state when the firm of Wm. H. Page & Co., was formed to carry it on in 1856, and the influence which this concern has exerted in developing it, may be gauged from the fact that the Wm. H. Page Wood Type Company (which succeeded the parent concern in 1876) now does more than half of all the American business in this line. The president of the company is Mr. S. T. Dauchy, the treasurer being Mr. Wm. H. Page, and the secretary Mr. Wm. E. Page. The company utilize spacious and well-equipped premises located at Nos. 286-296 Franklin street, and turn out their New Patented Process Type in large quantities, as the demand for it is brisk and increasing, requiring the operation of a large plant of improved machinery driven by a forty-horse engine, and the employment of forty assistants.

Fuller & Story, Insurance Agency, opposite Norwich Savings Society. Entrance No. 15 Shetucket Street, and 161 Main Street, Norwich, Conn.—The advantages of fire insurance have attained such general recognition that the question at the present time is not, "Shall I insure ?" but rather, "Where shall I place my insurance ?" This is also rapidly becoming true of life insurance as well, for ten men have their lives insured to-day where but one did a score of years ago. There seems to be no question but that the insurance of the future will be placed exclusively through agents, or at least very nearly so for a larger proportion is placed in this way every year, and the practice entails so many solid advantages that it is bound to continue to grow in popularity. Every agency which has been in operation a year or more must have some sort of a local reputation which will materially aid the public in deciding whether it is best to patronize it or not, and here is one powerful reason for the popularity noted, for it is much easier to investigate the standing of a local agency than to look up the record of several far away insurance companies, and it goes without saying that agents who have a high reputation for promptness and reliability will represent none but first class companies. We doubt if a better-known insurance agency than that conducted by Messrs. Fuller & Story can be found in this county, and we are positive that not one has a more enviable record to refer inquirers to. The enterprise had its inception about 1850, and is therefore the oldest agency in Norwich; it came under the control of Messrs. James E. Fuller, and J. Palmer Story in 1881. Both these gentlemen are natives of Norwich, and have a very extensive circle of acquaintances throughout this section. Their office is located opposite the Norwich Savings Society, and has one entrance at No. 15 Shetucket street, and another at No. 161 Main street. It has telephone connection, and communications can thus be quickly sent from any part of the city. The office hours are from 9 A. M. to 5 P. M., and any information relative to insurance matters will be cheerfully given on application. This firm have placed an immense amount of insurance to the entire satisfaction of all concerned and are prepared to write fire, life and accident policies in the leading companies at the lowest rates. As an indication of the facilities enjoyed we take pleasure in presenting the following list of companies represented : Ætna, Hartford; Pennsylvania, Philadelphia; Springfield, Springfield; American, New York City; American, Boston; Merchant's, Newark; Merchant's, Providence; Traders, Chicago; Grand, Philadelphia; Anglo-Nevada, San Francisco; Royal, Liverpool; London & Lancashire, Liverpool.

MUTUAL COMPANIES.

Windham County, Tolland County and Hartford County.

N. D. Sevin & Son, Druggists and Dispensing Chemists, 118 Main Street, Norwich, Conn.—It is well for any community to have such an enterprise as that conducted by Messrs. N. D. Sevin & Son within its borders, for this undertaking has been carried on for about twenty-five years and its management has been such as to fully justify the unbounded confidence reposed in it by the public The firm do a large wholesale drug business, and carry a very extensive and valuable stock, but it is in their capacity of dispensing chemists that they are the best known and most highly regarded by the general public. No intelligent person needs to be told how important it is that physicians' prescriptions should be compounded of materials of standard strength, in the most careful and accurate manner, and as Messrs. N. D. Sevin & Son have every facility at hand for the proper filling of such orders, and are in a position to guarantee the quality of the agents employed, it is but natural that many residents of this section should make it a practice to have all their prescriptions compounded at this well-equipped establishment, especially as all undue delay is avoided and moderate charges are uniformly made. Mr. N. D. Sevin is president of the State Board of Pharmacy and has been identified with his present establishment since 1865, at that time being a member of the firm of Lanman & Sevin. He became sole proprietor in 1879, and ten years later took his son, F. D. Sevin, who is a graduate of the New York College of Pharmacy, into partnership, under the existing firm name. The enterprise is a truly representative one, and all will unite in wishing it the high degree of success in the future it has earned by long and faithful service in the past.

The Buckingham, J. N. Weaver, Proprietor, Norwich, Conn.—It is seldom that a new hotel has met with the immediate success that has attended the popular Buckingham since it was opened to the public in the fall of 1889. The proprietors—both gentlemen of experience in the business—clearly foresaw that there was a demand in Norwich for a house where everything in its appointments would be strictly first-class, and where gentlemen could meet and enjoy a fine cigar, the finest liquors, or partake of a dinner such as is seldom served outside of Boston, New York, or the larger cities. The present building was taken therefore and entirely remodeled. The first floor, beautifully finished in oak, consists of a fine office about 40 × 40 feet with marble floor. In front is the gentlemen's reading room and in the rear is one of the handsomest and finest stocked bars in the State. From this floor we ascend to the cozy dining room seating about forty. Here the homelike character of the surroundings is at once apparent. Unlike the large, barnlike dining hall of many hotels the guest can enjoy a quiet meal promptly served by attentive waiters and from a bill of fare comprising all the luxuries of the season. In fact it is for the *cuisine* that the Buckingham is already noted, as each patron has given it the highest recommendation to his friends and there is no class who appreciate a finely cooked, well served dinner more than the travelling men, among whom the Buckingham is already famous. The two upper floors are devoted to sleeping apartments and consist of a number of well-ventilated rooms handsomely furnished with Brussels carpet and brass bedsteads with woven wire mattresses. Taken as a whole the popularity of this house is easily explained.

George R. Hannis, manufacturer of and wholesale and retail dealer in Cigars, Pipes, Snuffs, Tobaccos and Smokers' Articles, 18 Main Street, Norwich, Conn.—Perhaps some of our readers may have heard the story of the man who sent an anti-tobacco publication to Mark Twain and asked him to abandon the use of the "vile weed" so that his example would not encourage others to smoke. Mark's reply was in effect as follows: "All of us have some bad habits. Some poke their nose into other people's business and some use tobacco. I smoke." There is a good deal of sound philosophy in that view of the matter and we commend it to the attention of those who let one idea dominate their minds to the exclusion of everything else. Tobacco using is often spoken of as an expensive habit, but in no other way can so much genuine enjoyment be had at so small a cost. Call at the establishment conducted by Mr. Geo. R. Hannis at No. 18 Main street, and you will find he is prepared to furnish you with really excellent cigars at a very low figure. Mr. Hannis is a manufacturer and jobber of cigars and can therefore sell them at the lowest market rates, and at the same time guarantee that their quality shall prove as represented. He is also an extensive dealer in pipes, snuffs, tobaccos and smokers' articles in general, and offers so large and complete a stock that all tastes and all purses can be suited. He is a native of Springfield, Mass., a member of the Knights of Pythias, and established his present business in 1885.

Abraham Plaut, importer and dealer in Diamonds, Gold and Silver Watches, Optical Goods and Cutlery, Musical Merchandise, Strings, and Sheet Music, Pocket Books, Bags and Fancy Leather Goods, 200 Main Street, Norwich, Conn.—One of the oldest established and most highly regarded enterprises of the kind in this section of the State is that carried on by Mr. A. Plaut at No. 200 Main street, Perkins Block. This was inaugurated about a quarter of a century ago and has gained great popularity by reason of the energetic and straightforward business methods which have ever characterized its management. Mr. Plaut is a native of Germany, and has a large circle of friends in this city. His store is 65 × 20 feet in dimensions, and contains a fine and varied stock, comprising jewelry, watches and precious stones; music and musical merchandise and many other goods too numerous to mention, both a wholesale and retail business being done, and employment being given to two efficient assistants. Mr. Plaut is in a position to quote the very lowest prices on the various goods he handles, and careful buyers would do well to give him a call before purchasing as they will probably save money by so doing. An extensive brokerage business is done, liberal advances being made on personal property of every description and all business being transacted promptly, politely and satisfactorily to every patron who appreciates courtesy and fair dealing.

F. A. Wells & Co., the great New England Combination Clothiers, 84 Main Street, Norwich, Conn.—The importance of an announcement depends so largely upon the standing of the individual or the concern making it, that the simple statement that a certain house in this city assert that they are prepared to sell clothing cheaper than any other concern in Connecticut, bears but little weight until it is added that the name of this firm is F. A. Wells & Co.; and as this house has been in business here for a full score of years and has established a most enviable reputation for enterprise and fair dealing, any announcement that it may make is entitled to and will receive the respectful consideration of the purchasing public. Mr. F. A. Wells is a native of Waterbury, Vt., and has had a wide and varied experience in his present line of business, having carried it on for some five years before coming to Norwich. The premises utilized by him comprise two floors of the dimensions of 75 × 45 feet, and the stock on hand is exceptional insomuch as it includes not only a heavy and skillfully chosen assortment of ready made clothing, but also one of the most complete and desirable collections of harness, trunks, bags, carriages, etc., to be found in the State. Clothing suitable for all ages, all uses and all conditions of wear may be obtained at this popular store and in every instance at positively bottom prices. Employment is given to three efficient assistants and all callers are assured immediate and polite attention. The prices quoted in the trunk and bag department are also as low as the lowest, and the purchaser has the satisfaction of knowing that every article will prove strictly as represented.

P. G. Gordon, wholesale dealer in Woolen Rags, Paper Stock, Rubber and Old Metals, 118 Franklin Street, Norwich, Conn —Rags, paper stock, old metals and such "unconsidered trifles," may seem of but little importance to the casual observer, but the collection and sale of them forms one of the most useful of all branches of industry and exercises a very powerful influence on the price of stationery and other paper we use, the machinery we buy and the books and periodicals we read. The enterprise conducted by Mr. P. G. Gordon, at No. 118 Franklin street, is one of the longest established of the kind in Eastern Connecticut, it having been inaugurated very many years ago. It was for some time carried on by Mr. D. M. Dickinson, who was succeeded in 1884 by Messrs. Gordon & Stowe, the present proprietor assuming sole possession in August, 1889. Mr. Gordon utilizes two floors of the dimensions of 130 X 60 feet each, and carries an immense stock, comprising woolen rags, paper stock, rubber and old metals of all kinds. Employment is afforded to some eighteen assistants, and no house in the State in a similar line of business has a higher reputation for filling the very largest wholesale orders promptly, accurately, and in short—satisfactorily.

Pequot Brass Foundry Co., all kinds of Brass and Composition Castings, Pure Babbitt and Stevenson Metals constantly on hand. Office with Robert Brown, Pequot Building, Central Wharf, Norwich, Conn.—The demand for brass and composition castings is continually on the increase, and a well-equipped brass foundry is so useful an establishment to have in any manufacturing community that the enterprise conducted by the Pequot Brass Foundry Company is deserving of every encouragement as this is undoubtedly one of the best managed undertakings of the kind in Norwich and vicinity. It was founded in 1881 by Mr. Robert Brown and is carried on by a company constituted of Messrs. R. Brown, F. E. Green and F. E. Brown. The first named gentleman is a native of South Kingston, R. I., the second of Worcester, Mass., and the third of this city. The business manager of the company is Mr. F. E. Green, and the office is at the store of Mr. Robert Brown, Pequot Building, Central Wharf. The foundry occupies premises fifty feet square, and is supplied with the most improved facilities for the making of brass and composition castings at the shortest possible notice and in the most accurate manner. Pure Babbitt and Stevenson metals are kept constantly on hand and will be furnished in any desired quantity at the very lowest market rates, while order work and general jobbing will be done at uniformly moderate prices.

S. P. Keppler, Practical Tailor, Clothing Cut, Made and Trimmed in the Latest Styles. A fine assortment of Cassimeres, etc., on hand. Chambers 99 Main Street, Norwich, Conn.—Mr. S. P. Keppler does not charge the fancy prices which those who are fond of calling themselves "artist tailors," are so apt to quote, but his work is strictly first-class just the same, as will be agreed by any of our readers who are familiar with it. Although not calling himself an "artist tailor," Mr. Keppler *does* claim to be a "practical" tailor, and to cut, make and trim clothing in the very latest styles—a claim which we have no hesitation in saying is fully warranted by the facts in every respect. He is a native of Germany, and has carried on his present undertaking for more than a score of years, having founded it in 1869. The premises made use of are of the dimensions of 50 X 35 feet, and contain every facility for the prompt and accurate filling of orders, as well as an extensive and skillfully selected assortment of cassimeres and other fabrics of foreign and domestic manufacture. Mr. Keppler will make a suit or a single garment in a superior manner and at a very reasonable price, guaranteeing satisfaction as to fit, durability, etc. Particular attention is paid to the renovation of faded, unshapen or otherwise injured garments, these being cleansed, dyed and pressed so as to look practically as good as new, at charges within the means of all.

Laighton Brothers, Photographers, Shetucket Street, Norwich, Conn.—Those who look upon photography as a purely mechanical business (as some affect to do) must be puzzled to account for the vast difference noticeable in photographs made by those having equally good apparatus and having equal experience in its use, for although mechanical expertness will explain this difference to a certain extent, still after this has been given due consideration there remains a palpable discrepancy in the results attained by the two photographers which can only be satisfactorily accounted for in one way—one operator is an artist, the other is not. Compare the portraits made by Messrs. Laighton Brothers with those produced at certain other well equipped photograph galleries and an illustration will be given of what we mean. These other photographers may reproduce the features with mechanical exactness, they may make a highly finished piece of work in every respect—but that is just the trouble; it is nothing but "a piece of work" and not a portrait. Of course we do not mean to assert that Laighton Brothers are the only artistic photographers in town, but we do assert that they have very few equals and no superiors, while their prices are remarkably low considering the quality of the work. We speak of "Laighton Brothers" for it is by this firm-name that the enterprise to which we have reference is known to the public, but Mr. William S. Laighton is now sole proprietor, Mr. John Laighton having recently died. The present owner is a native of Farmington, N. H., and has been identified with the business since 1874. He employs two competent assistants and spares no pains to maintain the enviable reputation so long associated with the enterprise. Premises measuring 110 X 30 feet are occupied, conveniently located on Shetucket street, and photography in all its branches is carried on, orders being filled at short notice.

B. Shoninger & Co., Pianos and Organs, 101 Main St., Norwich.—Of all unsatisfactory investments that can be made, putting money into an inferior piano or organ is about the worst, for not only is such an instrument neither useful nor ornamental after a year or so, but the purchaser can not help thinking every time he sees it that had he only expended a few dollars more he could have secured something entirely and permanently satisfactory. We by no means approve of the policy adopted by some manufacturers of quoting fancy prices on their products, but still if one had to choose between paying $100 too much for a really first-class instrument, and paying $150 as the entire cost of one of the showy but worthless instruments far too common in the market, the former course would be decidedly the wiser one to take. Happily there is no need of taking either alternative, for the firm of B. Shoninger & Co., are prepared to supply strictly first class pianos and organs at prices as low as can be named on instruments of thoroughly dependable quality. At their spacious warerooms, No. 101 Main street, this concern show a full line of the productions of the famous B. Shoninger Piano and Organ Company, also the world-renowned Weber pianos, for which they are agents, and we can assure our readers that for quality of tone, combining sweetness and brilliancy, ease of action, susceptible to the most delicate touch, elegance of design, excellence of construction, fineness of finish, durability, and in fact all the qualities that go to make up a desirable instrument, these pianos and organs have no superior in this or any other country. The company operate an immense factory in New Haven, and have carried on business for forty years, during which they have attained a most enviable reputation for keeping faith with the public, and giving more genuine value for money received than any other piano and organ manufacturers in the country. Visitors are always welcome at the Norwich agency, and every opportunity will be given to try the instruments so as to enable deliberate, intelligent and satisfactory choice to be made, while every one sold is fully guaranteed for a term of six years.

C. E. Brady, Hack, Livery, Boarding and Sale Stable, 2 and 4 East Main Street, Norwich, Conn.—Norwich is famous for its long established business enterprises, but comparatively few of these can look back on so extended a career of usefulness as can that conducted by Mr. C. E. Brady on East Main street, near Bridge, for this is one of the oldest undertakings of the kind in this section of the State, having been founded very nearly a century ago. The present proprietor is a native of Canada, and has been in possession since 1880. He is very prominently identified with the stable business, owning an extensive establishment at Eastern Point in addition to the one already mentioned. Mr. Brady is proprietor of twenty-five horses, fifteen of which are kept at the East Main street stable, where there are also twenty to thirty carriages adapted to livery and hacking purposes, embracing landaus, English victorias, coupés, landaulettes, coupé rockaways, wagonettes carrying nine people, and every style of light carriage to be had. The cut above illustrates a pair of thoroughbreds, one of Mr. Brady's favorite teams. A very extensive hack, livery, boarding and sale business is done, and everything in and about the premises is kept in first-class condition, employment being given to four experienced assistants. Hacks will be furnished for parties, weddings, funerals and other occasions at very short notice, and at prices that are sure to prove satisfactory. The stable has telephone connection and orders sent thus or by mail are assured as prompt and painstaking attention as if given in person. Mr. Brady has some fine single and double teams for livery purposes, and those who want to go out on the road and "look as well as their neighbors," will find his turnouts just suited to their taste, as they will compare favorably with the large majority of private equipages.

Mrs. E. Cantle, Millinery and Fancy Goods, 23 Broadway, Norwich.—We are often told that the highest success in any given line of business is only possible to those who understand it thoroughly in every detail, and a very prominent illustration of this fact is that afforded by the leading position held by Mrs. E. Cantle, among the fashionable milliners of this State, for although this lady has been located in Norwich only about five years, she now conducts what is conceded to be the representative establishment of the kind in the city, the premises measuring 18x90 feet and being fitted up in the most tasteful and elaborate manner, while the stock on hand will compare favorably with that carried at many pretentious metropolitan stores. Mrs. Cantle was born in England, and had become an expert milliner when she arrived in this country in 1872, and opened a store near Rhinebeck, on the Hudson river, removing to Norwich at the date before given. Her business is steadily developing from year to year, and it is a noteworthy fact that her patronage is as select as it is extensive. A heavy stock of the very latest fashionable novelties in millinery goods is constantly carried, and silks, laces, flowers, velvets and trimmings in general are largely dealt in, as are also fancy and hair goods. Mrs. Cantle is agent for Butterick's Patterns, and always has a full assortment in stock, the latest numbers being promptly received, and the prices being identical with those quoted at the home office in New York. Custom millinery work is a very prominent feature of the business, and the popularity of this department is so great that a large force of skilled assistants are required during the busy season to attend to the many orders received.

G. F. PRENTIS,

✦ DENTIST ✦

91 Main Street.

Over Hislop, Porteous & Mitchell, Norwich.

W. H. Cardwell, Wholesale and Retail Groceries, Flour and Grain, 3 to 9 Market Street, Norwich, Conn. (See cut of building on opposite page.)—Were we asked to name half a dozen of the most prominent grocery houses in this section of the State, one of the first enterprises we would mention would be that conducted by Mr. W. H. Cardwell, for this was inaugurated fully thirty years ago and has long been looked upon as a representative undertaking of its kind, both as regards the methods employed in its management and its exceptional popularity throughout the community. The proprietor is a native of Montville, Conn., and has been identified with his present business since 1859, originally as a member of the firm of Cardwell & Tracy, later as Cardwell & Wait, and since 1883 as sole owner. He certainly needs no introduction to our Norwich readers, and his enterprising business methods have made him known by reputation at least, throughout this vicinity. The premises utilized are located at Nos. 3 to 9 Market street, and are so spacious as to admit of the carrying of an immense stock, composed of fancy and staple groceries in almost endless variety. This stock is as exceptional in quality as it is in magnitude, and it is generally conceded among consumers that goods obtained at this establishment are sure to prove entirely satisfactory. Mr. Cardwell does both a wholesale and retail business and is prepared to fill the most extensive orders without delay and at positively the lowest market rates. He employs four experienced and efficient assistants and every facility is at hand to ensure the prompt handling of goods.

SNELL BUSINESS COLLEGE, NOS. 99 TO 105 MAIN ST., NORWICH.

FRONTING MAIN AND MARKET STREETS.

This is a handsome building, made of Philadelphia pressed brick, with white granite casings, situated in the very heart of the city, commanding a perfect view of the harbor and the city's principal thoroughfare.

There is no dearth of "commercial colleges" in this country, but there are comparatively few institutions at which a really valuable and practical training in business principles and practices is to be obtained. The consequence is that in certain quarters a prejudice has grown up against commercial schools, they being condemned as pretentious and inefficient. This merely furnishes another illustration of the fact that an entire class is apt to be judged by the acts of individual members of it, and while such judgment may be entirely natural, it is none the less liable to result in injustice being done to certain persons or certain institutions. Take, for instance, the Snell Business College of Norwich, Ct., we believe that the more fully its workings are investigated the more clearly their common sense and practical results will be made manifest. Confined, as the present notice must be, to narrow limits, it is quite impossible to give an understandable summary even of the plan pursued here, but suffice it to say it is correct in principle, broad in scope and faithfully carried out in every detail. A personal visit will convey more solid information than could be given in pages of print, and Messrs. Snell and Burchard, the proprietors of the college, extend a cordial invitation to all interested to call and see for themselves. This enterprise was inaugurated in 1845 by Mr. Daniel W. Snell, who is a native of New Hampshire and had formerly carried on similar colleges in Worcester, Mass., and Trenton, N. J. In 1887 he became associated with Mr. Burchard,

who was born in this city and is very generally and favorably known here. The institution is rapidly gaining in popularity and influence, and already ranks with the leading business colleges of New England. There were 169 scholars the last school year and there will be more than 200 during the year ensuing. The course comprises instruction in single and double entry book keeping, business mathematics, plain and ornamental penmanship, stenography, verbatim court reporting, business correspondence, political economy, commercial geography, languages, etc. The college is conveniently and pleasantly located at No. 99 Main street, eight spacious apartments being utilized. The terms of tuition are reasonable and the corps of instructors is adequate and competent.

TERMS, AS FOLLOWS:

DAY SESSION.

REGULAR COMMERCIAL COURSE, COMPLETE,

$80.00   Eighty Dollars   **$80.00**

This includes all text-books and stationery, and embraces every study necessary for a thorough knowledge of business. Time unlimited.

STENOGRAPHIC AND TYPE-WRITING COURSE,

From correspondence to verbatim reporting,

$35.00   Thirty five Dollars   **$35.00**

PENMANSHIP—BUSINESS AND ORNAMENTAL,

In its entirety,

$25.00   Twenty-Five Dollars   **$25.00**

EVENING SESSION.

REGULAR COURSE—TIME, SIX MONTHS,

$30.00   Thirty Dollars   **$30.00**

STENOGRAPHIC AND TYPE-WRITING COURSE,

Complete, for

$30.00   Thirty Dollars   **$30.00**

PENMANSHIP—BUSINESS AND ORNAMENTAL,

$15.00   Fifteen Dollars   **$15.00**

NOTE.—Remember, these prices are for both tuition and stationery, and time unlimited.

Catalogue Mailed Free.

SENIOR PRACTICAL DEPARTMENT.

George A. Smith, dealer in Fine China, Glassware and Crockery, headquarters for Royal Worcester and French China for Decorating, 17 Main Street, Carroll Block, Norwich.—The store recently opened by Mr. George A. Smith at No. 17 Main street, Carroll Block, is one of the most attractive to visit in the city, for an exceptionally handsome and complete stock of fine china, glassware, and crockery is there open to inspection, and those in search of the latest and most artistic novelties may save time and trouble by coming to this well-appointed establishment in the first place. Mr. Smith makes a specialty of Royal Worcester and French china for decorating, and is determined to maintain the reputation already won of making his store the headquarters for such goods. Within our necessarily narrow limits it is quite impossible to give an adequate idea of a stock so large and varied as his, and even could we spare space to catalogue it, the result would be of but comparatively slight utility to our readers, for the assortment is constantly changing, although of course certain standard styles in white and colored goods are always kept on hand. Mr. Smith enjoys very favorable relations with manufacturers and is in a position to quote the very lowest market rates on all the articles in which he deals, whether they be of foreign or domestic origin. His stock is by no means confined to the higher priced goods, but on the contrary includes practically all grades of china, glass ware and crockery, so that all tastes and all purses can be easily and entirely suited.

J. F. Conant, manufacturer and dealer in Cigars, Tobacco, Snuffs and Pipes, and Smokers' Articles, 235 Main Street, Norwich.—There is but one sure way of distinguishing a good cigar and that is to smoke it, for in spite of the claims of self-styled "experts," we question if there be a man living who can infallibly judge by any other means. Examination will tell whether a cigar is well made or not, and whether it is well seasoned or not; but beyond this it avails but little, and therefore the smoker has one surety that he will not be imposed upon, and that is the reputation of the dealer from whom he buys. Mr. J. F. Conant has long had the name of selling thoroughly satisfactory cigars at moderate prices, and this name is so well deserved that we feel that we can do our readers no greater service than to call their attention to this gentleman's establishment at No. 235 Main street, for here may be found a remarkably complete assortment of cigars, pipes, tobaccos, and smokers' articles of all kinds, and the prices are as satisfactory as are the goods themselves. The store is 45×20 feet in dimensions and contains, among other things, as fine an assortment of genuine meerschaum goods as this city can show. Mr. Conant has carried on this business since 1879, at that time succeeding Mr. Frank B. Conant who had started it in 1876. The present owner is a native of Massachusetts and is connected with the Odd Fellows. He makes a specialty of the "Louise" cigar, which is a celebrated and popular brand, of remarkably uniform quality. Employment is given to two assistants and callers are assured prompt and polite attention.

I. W. Carpenter, Agent for the Massachusetts Mutual Life Insurance Company, of Springfield, Mass. No. 3 Richard's Building, Norwich.—Public sentiment concerning life insurance has reached a point where it is no longer a question of "Shall I insure or not?" but rather "In what company shall I take out a policy?" This is a decided change from the time when life insurance was regarded as immoral—a tempting of Providence and all that; but it is in line with the growing liberality noticeable on all sides and shows that broader views of existence are held throughout the community. Doubtless the Massachusetts Mutual Life Insurance Company has done much towards attracting attention to the advantages of life insurance, for this company has carried on operations for nearly forty years and has disbursed millions of dollars in the payment of death claims and dividends. The guiding policy of the company is indicated by the following sentence from the last annual statement—" What the insuring public want is absolute security and after that end is attained, to receive what dividends can be reasonably paid them." Certainly no more conservative a position as to the functions of a life insurance company could be held, and it is not to be wondered at that an investment in the Massachusetts Mutual is considered by able business men to be "as good as gold." The company has had an agency in this city for about six years. Mr. I. W. Carpenter having been resident agent from the beginning. A better choice could not have been made, for Mr. Carpenter is universally known throughout this section and has been very successful in extending the company's business in this vicinity. He was born in Norwich and has held various public offices, among them that of Mayor of the city. Mr. Carpenter's office is at No. 3 Richard's building, 91 Main street, where he will be happy to give all information desired on application. We give below the financial standing of the company at the last accounting:

RECEIPTS IN 1889.

Premiums,	$1,913,230.88
Interest and Rents,	505,125.90
Profit and Loss,	39,495.05
Total Receipts,	**$2,457,851.83**

DISBURSEMENTS.

Death Claims (less $25,495 Re-Insurance), ..	$585,402.00
Matured Endowments,	102,589.00
Surplus returned to policy holders in Dividends—	225,777.57
Surrendered and Canceled Policies,	178,240.72
Total payments to Policy Holders,	**$1,092,009.29**
Commissions, Salaries, and other expenses,	473,558.92
Taxes and Licenses paid Massachusetts and other Insurance Departments,	$30,422.94
Taxes on Real Estate,	5,246.25
	35,669.19
Expenses on Real Estate,	20,798.84
Re-Insurance,	45,668.68
Total Disbursements,	**$1,668,014.86**

ASSETS.

First Mortgage Loans on Real Estate,	$3,576,257.42
Loans secured by Collaterals,	701,200.00
Loans on Company's Policies in force,	319,402.00
Massachusetts Armory Loan Bonds,	110,000.00
City, County, Township and other Bonds,	843,152.60
Gas and Water Bonds,	304,850.00
National Bank Stocks,	83,850.00
Railroad Bonds,	1,794,116.16
Railroad and other Stocks,	775,516.00
Real Estate,	459,218.08
Premium Note on Policies in force,	547,027.02
Cash on hand and in Bank,	201,017.27
Premiums in course of collection (less cost of collection),	122,485.44
Deferred Premiums (less cost of collection),	207,065.74
Interest and Rents accrued,	132,079.90
Total Assets,	**$10,415,817.64**

LIABILITIES.

Reserve by Massachusetts Standard,	$9,502,188.00
Claims for Death Losses and Matured Endowments in process of adjustment,	23,828.85
Unpaid Dividends,	30,358.80
Premiums paid in advance,	2,099.98
Total Liabilities,	**$9,558,475.63**
Surplus by the Massachusetts Standard,	**$857,342.01**

Number of Policies issued in 1889, 4,113, insuring....	$15,032,300.00
Number of Policies in force December 31, 1889, 40,626, insuring (including Reversionary additions)...	56,320,568.00

SPRINGFIELD, Mass., Jan. 15, 1890.

The undersigned have carefully examined the cash, securities and balances of The Massachusetts Mutual Life Insurance Company, and find the same to agree with the above statement.

H. S. Hyde,)
John R. Redfield, } Auditors.
E. D. Metcalf,)

M. V. B. Edgerly, President.   John A. Hall, Secretary.
Henry S. Lee, Vice President.   Oscar B. Ireland, Actuary.

The Ponemah Cotton Mills, Taftville, Norwich.—We frequently hear of the phenomenally rapid growth of western communities and the slow and painful development of eastern towns and cities, and the comparison is made invariably to the disadvantage of the residents of the latter section, but leaving out of the question the significant fact that in most cases western development is due in a great measure to eastern capital, we can show instances of rapid growth here in the east, which are all the more noteworthy from the fact that the results attained are as permanent as they are phenomenal. Our Norwich readers will not have to go away from home to find a prominent case in point for in the village of Taftville, about three miles from the centre of the city, is located what is to all appearance a small city, containing many handsome buildings and giving every evidence of healthful development and solid prosperity. Yet, a score of years ago, there was hardly a house to be seen here, and that such is not the case to day is due to the far sighted enterprise of those who originated and put into practical operation the vast undertaking carried on by the Ponemah Cotton Mills. These mills form the second largest cotton factory in the Union and probably in the world, and represent the expenditure of hundreds of thousands of dollars for buildings alone, to say nothing of the enormously costly plant of machinery connected with them. They are located on the Shetucket River, and the building of the dam was commenced in 1866, the machinery first being put in operation in 1871. The mill is of such immense size that figures give but an inadequate idea of its proportions, but some conception of their magnitude may be gained from the fact that the total length is nearly one-third of a mile. Various stores, store-houses and buildings of varied utility are used in more or less remote connection with the enterprise, and the company own some 170 tenement houses which are leased to some of the 1500 operatives. The corporation has a capital of two millions, and manufactures a choice quality of cotton goods which are known and appreciated throughout the United States. Carrying on operations on so immense a scale and having the most improved facilities of all kinds, it goes without saying that the greatest possible economy is attained in production, thus putting the company in a position to quote positively the lowest market rates, while the processes of manufacture are so thoroughly systematized and so carefully supervised as to result in a product not often equalled as regards uniform excellence. Nearly half a million dollars is paid in wages every year and 120,-000 spindles are operated; there being some 6,500 bales of cotton consumed and no less than 20,000,000 yards or nearly 11,400 miles of goods turned out annually.

J. F. Cosgrove & Co., wholesale and retail dealers in Boots, Shoes and Rubbers, Fine Goods a Specialty, Orders by Mail or Express promptly filled, 206 Main street, Norwich, Conn.—Although there are many purchasers of boots and shoes who pride themselves on their expertness in judging the quality of such goods from a merely superficial examination, there are also many who recognize the fact that but little real dependence can be placed upon the results of such examination; the real insurance held by the retail buyer against deception being that afforded by the character of the concern with whom he deals. The old proverb assures us that "A good name is better than great riches," and a business firm is very apt to realize that in the long run a good name is essential to the building up of a permanent trade of any magnitude. The popularity of the establishment conducted by Messrs. J. F. Cosgrove & Co. is of course due to some extent to the enterprise the firm show in offering the very latest fashionable novelties, etc., but it is principally owing to the fact that the community know that whatever representations are made here may be implicitly relied upon. This business was founded in 1877 by Mr. J. F. Cosgrove, who became associated with Mr. D. W. Cosgrove under the present firm name in 1879. Both partners give close attention to the business, and are too generally known in this vicinity to call for extended

mention. The store is located at No. 206 Main street, and is 75×25 feet in dimensions, being finely fitted up throughout. Both a wholesale and retail business is done in boots, shoes and rubbers, a specialty being made of fine goods. Orders by mail or express will be promptly filled, and the employment of three competent assistants ensures immediate attention to every caller. A very heavy and varied stock is carried, embracing foot-wear of every description, and both the prices and the goods are such as to give entire satisfaction to the most critical purchasers.

The Norwich Savings Society, Norwich.—If there be a local corporation in which the residents of Norwich have especial reason to take pride, it is certainly the Norwich Savings Society for since the formation of this company in May, 1824, it has made a record which distinguishes it among even New England institutions of like character,—and New England stands second to no portion of the world as regards the scope and efficiency of her savings banks. Such institutions, however well managed, are helpless without the aid and co operation of the people, and no small part of the pride which a citizen takes in the Norwich Savings Society is due to his appreciating the fact that its success is proof positive that a large proportion of his fellow citizens have the disposition and the ability to put aside a portion of their earnings, and the discrimination to confide their savings to a bank conservatively, yet progressively managed. Few enterprises are altogether beneficent in their workings, but it seems to us as if well-managed savings banks should be numbered among these few, for to our mind their influence is distinctly and entirely beneficial. They inculcate economy, put the advantages of prudence into practical form, divert money from unprofitable to profitable channels and to a great extent counteract the American tendency towards extravagance. A man who has a few hundreds of his own earning deposited in a savings bank must be a better citizen than he otherwise would be, for he feels more secure regarding the future, has a clearer conception of the rights of property, and to some degree at least understands the fundamental principles of finance. Therefore without attempting to deny that the Norwich Savings Society was organized on a business basis and not solely for the public good, it may still be consistently asserted that few distinctively charitable enterprises have proved of equal benefit to the community. Many leading merchants and manufacturers are members of the society, and their names and standing, taken in connection with the past record of the bank, afford positive assurance that the institution will continue to be ably and conservatively managed. There is now held on deposit about nine millions of dollars, and that the disposal of this vast sum of money is in competent hands a perusal of the following list will show:

Norwich Bleaching Dyeing and Printing Company, Norwich, Conn.—So vast an enterprise as that conducted by the Norwich Bleaching, Dyeing and Printing Company, is not to be adequately described within the limited space at our command, for even a single department of the company's business would require several columns of print to put its operations clearly before our readers ; so that all we shall endeavor to do is to convey some idea of the magnitude of the undertaking and the important influence it exerts upon the prosperity of this section. At the outset, it may be stated that the company carry on one of the largest establishments of the kind in America, and some idea of the immensity and costliness of the plant in use may be gained from the fact that the capital employed amounts to half a million of dollars. The enterprise had its inception in 1842, being started by the Norwich Bleaching and Calendering Company ; the existing style being adopted in 1883. Mr. H. H Osgood is president of the company, Mr. Charles Bard being vice-president, and Mr. J. Hunt Smith, secretary and treasurer, these gentlemen being associated on the board of directors with Messrs. H. B. Norton, A. H. Young and Lucius Briggs. It will be seen that the company's interests are in the hands of representative business men, and indeed the entire enterprise is representative to an exceptional degree. The premises utilized cover several acres and include twelve large buildings which are equipped throughout with the most efficient and improved machinery, while employment is given to more than 400 operatives ; the annual production of cotton goods amounting to over 60,000,000 yards—(the last six months 33,347,994 yards were finished)—or more than enough to encircle the earth at the equator ! Such enormous productive facilities carry with them the ability to meet all honorable competition, and it is very generally known that the Norwich Bleaching, Dyeing and Printing Company are always prepared to quote the lowest market rates and to fill the heaviest orders at comparatively short notice. They produce a great variety of original and attractive styles and their goods are shipped to all sections of the Union, being popular alike with dealers and consumers.

C. D. Browning & Co., Dry Goods, Clothing, Carpets, Paper Hangings and Boots and Shoes, 253 Central Avenue, and Groceries, Provisions and Drugs at 35 Sixth Street, Norwich, Conn Branch Stores at Hallville (Preston) and Flanders (East Lyme).—The firm of C. D. Browning & Co., doing business at No. 253 Central avenue and No. 35 Sixth street, rank with the most popular dealers in dry goods, carpets, clothing, groceries, provisions, boots, shoes, etc., etc., in this vicinity, and this popularity is directly due to the thoroughness with which the firm carry out every detail of their business. The Norwich double store is one of three established under their management, one being carried on at Hallville and another at East Lyme. The undertaking in question was established over fifty years ago by S. and A. S. Prentice, who were succeeded in 1849 by Mr. C. D. Browning. In 1869 Mr. T. A. Perkins was admitted to the firm since which date business has been conducted under the style of C. D. Browning & Co. These gentlemen are both well known throughout the community as reliable and enterprising business men. Mr. Browning is a native of North Stonington, and Mr. Perkins of East Lyme. Owing to the extensive business transacted two adjoining stores are occupied—the larger at 253 Central avenue is 60×40 feet in size and contains a large stock of dry and fancy goods, clothing, carpets, boots and shoes and paper hangings. The store at 35 Sixth street adjoining, is well stocked with groceries, provisions, drugs, etc., etc. Orders by mail or telephone promptly delivered to any part of the city. Employment is given to several efficient assistants and patrons are sure of receiving immediate, polite and painstaking attention at all times. Messrs. C. D. Browning & Co.'s facilities are of the best, and as before intimated, they not only furnish first class goods but quote the very lowest market prices in every department.

Norwich Belt Mfg. Company, Tanners and manufacturers of Oak Leather Belting. Tanned and Raw Hide Lace Leather, Rubber and Cotton Belting, Leather and Mill Supplies, 35 Water Street, Norwich; Branch, 33 North Canal Street, Chicago.—No experienced manufacturer needs to be told of the advantages of using first-class belting for he has had ample opportunity to learn from practical experience that " the best is the cheapest," in more ways than one. Appearances are as deceitful in belting as in many other things and the only sure way to obtain goods that will give entire satisfaction is to deal with a house that has the facilities, the determination and the ability to produce belting equal to any in the market. Such a house is the Norwich Belt Manufacturing Company, and as this business was established as early as 1845 it is not at all surprising that the enterprise should be universally known throughout this section of the country. The present proprietors assumed control in 1873 and have materially added to the high reputation the undertaking previously enjoyed. Mr. H. H. Gallup and Mr. Frank Ulmer are too generally known to render extended personal mention necessary, and that their methods are appreciated is evidenced by the fact of the annual sales exceeding $300,000 in amount. The manufacture of oak leather belting is very extensively carried on, a spacious and well-equipped tannery being maintained at Greenville, and a very large warehouse being occupied at No. 35 Water street, Norwich. Here five floors, of the dimensions of 110 × 20 feet are utilized, and an immense stock is carried, comprising leather belting, tanned and raw hide lace leather, rubber and cotton belting, leather and mill supplies, etc. A branch establishment is located at No. 33 North Canal street, Chicago, and employment is given to about sixty hands. A specialty is made of dynamo belting, but all kinds and all grades can be supplied in quantities to suit, at bottom rates and without delay.

Wauregan Stables, D. S. Tweedy, Proprietor (E. D. Clark's old stand), Hack, Livery, Boarding and Feeding Stables ; Orders for Carriages or Hacks, for any train, or at any hour of the night, by Mail, Telegraph or Telephone, promptly attended to. Conveyances for Picnics, Base Ball Parties, etc. Particular attention paid to Funerals. Nos. 14, 16, 18 and 20 Bath Street, Norwich, Conn.—The numerous delightful drives in the vicinity of Norwich, and the fondness of the people as a whole for this healthful form of recreation, have resulted in the establishment of many livery stables which range through all grades of good, bad and indifferent. The enjoyment of one who goes upon the road is so directly dependent upon the character of the team he has, that it is absurd not to use some discrimination in the placing of the order, and as this book will be widely circulated among those who visit Norwich occasionally but are not thoroughly acquainted with the merits of the various local stables, we take pleasure in aiding them in such discrimination by calling their attention to an establishment at which the very best turnouts may be obtained at moderate rates—the Wauregan Stables, located at Nos 14, 16, 18 and 20 Bath street. These were opened a quarter of a century ago by Mr. E Osgood, and came into the possession of the present proprietor, Mr. D. S. Tweedy, in 1883. Mr. Tweedy employs six assistants, and does an extensive and steadily growing business. The livery department is probably the most important, but an extensive hacking business is also done, and boarding and baiting are prominent and popular features. The proprietor spares no trouble to conduct what may truly be called a Metropolitan establishment, or at least one run on Metropolitan principles, for teams may be had at all hours at very short notice, and the prices quoted are uniformly moderate. These stables certainly deserve their popularity.

C. E. CHANDLER,

CIVIL ENGINEER AND SURVEYOR

161 MAIN STREET, NORWICH.

Jewett Bros., dealers in Coal, 154 Main and 58 Thames Street, Norwich.—In theory it makes but little difference as to where an order for coal is placed under existing arrangements, but in practice it makes a good deal and many residents of Norwich and vicinity have discovered that the firm of Jewett Brothers are in a position to offer particular inducements to coal consumers, whether their wants be large or small. Messrs. Jewett Brothers handle both Lackawanna and Lehigh coal, and maintain an extensive yard at No. 59 Thames street, where a very heavy stock is carried at all times. The office is located at No. 154 Main street, and orders left there or at the yard are assured equally prompt and painstaking attention. In the coal business, above almost all others, the facilities for delivery are of prime importance and a great part of the popularity of the concern in question among all classes of consumers is due to their ability to fill orders accurately and within the time promised. But little inconvenience generally attends delay in the delivery of groceries or other staple commodities, but with coal it is different, and such of our readers as have experienced the consequences of delay in this connection will appreciate a service which is at once prompt and uniformly reliable.

L. L. Chapman, Hack, Livery, Boarding and Feed Stable, 160 West Main Street, Norwich, Conn.—We have no doubt but what it would surprise the large majority of our readers to learn how heavy a sum of money is expended for horse hire per year in Norwich alone, and yet it is obvious that the amount must be very considerable, for there are many livery stables in the city and the cost of carrying these on must aggregate a very large sum. Generally speaking, the money spent in horse hire is well invested, for it is apt to yield a big dividend of pleasure and health and it would unquestionably be better for the community as a whole if much more were expended in this direction. One of the oldest established public stables in this vicinity is that carried on by Mr. L. L. Chapman at No. 160 West Main street, this enterprise having been started more than forty years ago by Mr. Bentley. The present proprietor assumed control in 1889, and has not only maintained but even added to the high reputation so long associated with the undertaking. He is a native of Ledyard, Conn., and gives close personal attention to the filling of orders, while employing sufficient assistance to enable him to execute all commissions at short notice. Mr. Chapman does a hack, livery, boarding and feed business and makes a specialty of furnishing desirable and safe teams, single and double, at uniformly moderate prices. Horses will be taken to board at a reasonable charge, and at no stable in the city are they more sure of comfortable accommodations and satisfactory food and care.

A. T. Converse, Iron and Steel, 23 Commerce Street, Norwich, Conn.—It is obvious that there must be a great demand for iron and steel in this city and vicinity, for manufacturing is so largely carried on here that the consumption of these metals is very extensive. Among the leading dealers in iron and steel, not only in this city but in the entire State, mention should properly be made of Mr. A. T. Converse, for this gentleman has been identified with this line of business for about forty years, having begun operations in 1850. The premises made use of are located at No. 23 Commerce street and comprise four floors of the dimensions of 85 × 40 feet, with one of the best wharves in Norwich. A very large, varied and valuable stock is constantly carried, comprising sable bar iron, Akron calendered shafting, galvanized and black sheet iron, Norway iron, black diamond cast and silver steel, machinery, tire and caulking steel, etc. The bulk of the trade is in pig iron, but a large business is also done in the varieties mentioned above and also in supplying builders with special bolts and forgings. Mr. Converse employs six assistants and is prepared to fill all orders at short notice and at bottom rates. He has extensive storage facilities at his disposal and goods of all kinds will be stored for a long or short period at a moderate charge.

Sibley Machine Co., manufacturers of Paper Engines, Dusters, Rag and Paper Cutters, Mill Gearing, Shafting, Hangers, Water Pipes; Jobbing of all kinds, and Castings at short notice. Agents for Hunt's Double-Acting Turbine Water Wheel, 48 Franklin Street, Norwich, Conn.—The manufacture of paper has long been one of the great industries of the country, and of late years it has developed with a rapidity so remarkable as to be little short of marvelous. Paper making machinery has now reached a very high stage of perfection, and so important an influence does the machinery used exert upon the quality and the cost of the product that no paper manufacturer can afford to dispense with the latest improved labor-saving devices. The Sibley Machine Company make a specialty of the manufacture of paper engines, dusters, rag and paper cutters, and their products have attained an unsurpassed reputation among practical men throughout the country. The company operate a well chosen plant of machinery, employ twenty skilled assistants, and turn out machines which are thoroughly well made in every part and hence are reliable under all circumstances. The prices quoted are as low as is consistent with the use of suitable materials, etc., and the company's machines are rapidly coming into general use. The enterprise was started in 1876 by Mr. Rufus Sibley, and has become one of the representative undertakings of this city. The company also manufacture mill gearing, shafting, hangers, water pipe, etc., and are prepared to make castings or to do jobbing of all kinds at short notice. They are agents for Hunt's celebrated double-acting turbine water wheel and can supply the same at manufacturers' rates. The shop is located at No. 48 Franklin street, and telephone connection is had.

Hirsch & Co., Clothiers and Furnishers, 47 Shetucket Street, Norwich, 23 Bank Street, New London.—It would be hard to name a line in which greater energy and enterprise are displayed than in the ready-made clothing business, and indeed it would seem as if the most able and progressive merchants chose this branch of commerce, judging from the extent to which it has been developed of late years. Many persons who would once have laughed at the idea of wearing ready-made clothing, now do so from choice, and this change of sentiment is not due to any lowering of the standard of taste, but to the fact that the ready-made garments of to-day are practically equal to custom clothing, while being much less expensive. Of course this is true only of first-class ready-made clothing, but such can easily be obtained by visiting the right establishment, and we believe it would be impossible to find one nearer "right" in every respect than that conducted by Messrs. Hirsch & Co., at Norwich and New London. Here the goods are "right," the prices are "right," and the service is "right," and this combination of good points is so exceptional and so popular, that it is not at all surprising a large and constantly increasing patronage should be enjoyed. The premises measure 75×35 feet, and contain a heavy and varied stock of clothing and furnishings, in which the latest fashionable novelties are fully represented while at the same time room is left for the carrying of complete lines of more staple goods. Employment is given to three efficient assistants and callers are attended to with courtesy and despatch. This firm have another store, in New London, and have carried on operations for about sixteen years there and eight in Norwich, during which time they have built up an enviable reputation for fair dealing and enterprise.

Eaton, Chase & Co. (successors to A. W. Prentice & Co.,) Hardware, wholesale and retail, manufacturers of Breed's Cotton and Linen Lines and Factory Banding, No. 7 Commerce Street, Norwich, Conn.—Business enterprises which have been carried on for a quarter of a century are not common ; those which were inaugurated a half-century ago are still more rare, and those which were founded a full century ago are so exceptional as to deserve special mention ; but when an undertaking is found which has been successfully conducted for more than a century and a quarter, it should be given extended and favorable notice and we only regret that the limitations of space forbid our presenting a detailed history of the business carried on by Messrs. Eaton, Chase & Co. for this was established in 1764 and has ever been conducted in a manner which has made it truly representative in the fullest sense of the word. The founder was Mr. Gersham Breed, who was succeeded by Messrs. Jesse and Simon Breed, and they gave place to Messrs. Joseph and John Breed, who were succeeded by Messrs. John Breed & Co., this firm being formed in 1840 and consisting of Messrs. John Breed and A. W. Prentice. In 1856, the style, Breed, Prentice & Co. was adopted, and in 1864 the firm of A. W. Prentice & Co. assumed control, this style being continued until February, 1889, when Mr. Prentice retired and the existing firm was formed. It is constituted of Messrs. L. S. Eaton, A H. Chase, L. E. Stockwell and D. H. Hough ; the first named gentleman having been connected with the hardware trade since 1870. A very extensive wholesale and retail hardware trade is carried on, the premises in use comprising four floors of the dimensions of 45 x 90 feet, and being filled with a most varied assortment made up of hardware, cutlery, mechanics' tools, electrical supplies, firearms, ammunition, mill supplies and other commodities, including a full line of cordage. The firm operate a well equipped rope-walk and manufacture Breed's cotton and linen lines and factory banding, so well and favorably known in the market. Employment is given to thirteen competent assistants at the store and every order is assured prompt and careful attention, the present concern being fully prepared to maintain the honorable reputation so long associated with the enterprise under their charge.

C. B. Rogers & Co., makers of the latest improved Wood-working Machinery. Warerooms : 109 Liberty Street, New York ; 54 Oliver Street, Boston. Principal Office and Manufactory: Norwich, Conn.—One does not have to be a mechanic in order to understand the importance of having wood-working machinery thoroughly made of the very best material, for the high speed at which such machinery is run and the tremendous strains consequently brought to bear upon it would soon injure or destroy imperfect appliances. The unequalled reputation held by the productions of Messrs. C. B. Rogers & Co., among practical wood-workers throughout the world is due not less to the perfection of the workmanship noticeable in the machinery made by this firm, than to the excellence of its design, and it is gratifying to point out a local enterprise which has done so much to make American ingenuity and reliability appreciated in other lands. The concern has been awarded first prizes at Paris, London, Vienna, Sidney, and other foreign trade centres, as well as at expositions held throughout this country, and their trade extends to all parts of the United States and also to Australia, Mexico, South America, etc. The business was founded in 1836 by Messrs. J. Fay & Co., and was located in Keene, N. H., a branch afterwards being started at Worcester, Mass. In 1860 the entire plant, etc., were transferred to this city, and three years later the existing company was incorporated, Mr. C. B. Rogers being president and Mr. Lyman Gould, secretary, the latter gentleman being chosen president on the death of Mr. Rogers in 1871. Mr. R. W. Perkins is secretary and general manager, and the board of directors is made up of Messrs. L. Gould, George W. Gould, R. W. Perkins, W. V. Gould, George Pierce, Edward Chappell and Asa Backus. The company maintain a most completely equipped factory and employ about 125 skilled mechanics. They manufacture the very latest improved wood-working machinery and are continually bringing out new machines, embodying original and valuable features. Among those of recent date may be mentioned the new inside moulder, and the fast feed flooring machine, and as the company publish a fine illustrated catalogue of their productions, those wishing information concerning these or any of the machines made can easily obtain the same on application. Warerooms are maintained at No. 109 Liberty Street, New York, and No. 54 Oliver Street, Boston, and every order is assured prompt and painstaking attention; the principal office and manufactory being located in this city.

O. H. Reynolds, Hack, Livery and Boarding Stables, Nos. 55, 57 and 59 Shetucket Street, Norwich, Conn.—The claim that the hack, livery and boarding stables conducted by Mr. O. H. Reynolds, and located at Nos. 55, 57 and 59 Shetucket street, have for leading and favorable mention among the representative public stables of Norwich and vicinity, will not be disputed by those at all familiar with the facts in the case, for during the half century that the enterprise in question has been carried on it has made an unsurpassed record for efficiency and reliability The present proprietor is a native of Salem, Conn., and has had control ever since 1867, he being one of the best known stable keepers in the State. The premises utilized are spacious and well arranged, and include a fine two-story brick building, of the dimensions of 100 × 75 feet. Employment is given to about ten assistants, and despite the magnitude of the business, orders are filled with a promptness and care which will be looked for in vain at many much smaller establishments. Mr. Reynolds does an immense livery business, and is prepared to furnish single or double teams at any time, and at uniformly moderate rates. He recognizes the fact that to hold a desirable class of trade he must furnish strictly first-class turnouts, and we believe his teams will compare favorably with an equal number taken at random from the best private stables of this city. Hacks will be supplied for weddings, balls, funerals or other public occasions, careful and competent drivers being provided. Unsurpassed boarding facilities are offered at this stable.

DRY AND FANCY GOODS,

DOMESTIC SEWING MACHINES,

19 Broadway, Norwich,   -   Wauregan Hotel Building.

A. D. Lathrop, Teaming of all Kinds, 333 Main Street, Norwich.—In a work devoted to a consideration of the business interests of a section, it is fitting that prominent mention should be made of such an enterprise as that conducted by Mr. A. D. Lathrop, for this has much to do with the facilitation of business and has proved of great utility to Norwich merchants and manufacturers, during the seventeen years that it has been in operation. Mr. Lathrop is a native of Lebanon, and is so widely and favorably known in this city and vicinity, that extended personal mention is quite uncalled for. He does teaming of all kinds and has an equipment which enables him to fill every order at short notice and at prices which cannot fail to prove satisfactory to every reasonable customer. This equipment includes six large teams besides smaller wagons, and is kept in excellent condition at all times,—a fact which has much to do with its uniform efficiency. Employment is given to from seven to nine men, and goods are handled carefully as well as rapidly. The office is located corner Shetucket and Market streets, and orders left in person or sent by mail or messenger are assured immediate and painstaking attention.

C. C. Bliss, Jeweler, 126 Main Street, Norwich, Conn.— It is perfectly natural, of course, that buyers of jewelry should give the preference to old established houses when placing their orders, for it is obvious that great frauds are possible in the handling of such articles and although the integrity of comparatively new concerns may not be questioned in the slightest degree, still such firms can certainly offer no *greater* advantages than can those of long standing, and the probability is they offer less. Then again, a jeweler who has long carried on business in one community, gets to know the tastes of the people so thoroughly that his stock contains few, if any, articles which will not be thought desirable, whereas a dealer who has not had the opportunity to acquire this knowledge will, of necessity, encumber his premises with goods for which there is practically no local demand. A good idea of what we mean by the first-mentioned stock may be gained by visiting the store of Mr. C. C. Bliss, at No. 126 Main street, for this gentleman carries a very large and varied assortment, and has an experience extending over more than a quarter of a century to guide him in catering to Norwich patrons. The business conducted by him was founded many years ago by Mr. E. T. Huntington, and the present proprietor (who is a native of Norwich) assumed control about 1862. The premises utilized are elegantly fitted up, and have an area of between 800 and 1000 square feet. The stock comprises the very latest novelties in jewelry and similar goods, and it would certainly seem as if all tastes and all purses could be suited from it, for it is so varied and so complete in every department that merely to catalogue it would exhaust many times our available space. Employment is given to two efficient assistants, and custom work and repairing are assured prompt and skillful attention at moderate charges.

The Chelsea File Works, manufacturers of Exclus v Hand-Cut Files and Rasps, Norwich, Conn.—The products of the Chelsea File Works have been on the market for over a quarter of a century, for this enterprise was inaugurated in 1863 by a stock company, one of the members of which was Mr. H. L. Butts, who since 1876 has been sole proprietor. Mr. Butts is a native of Mansfield, Conn., and is one of the oldest residents of Norwich, having lived in this city ever since 1839. He is very widely known throughout this section, and the products of his factory are popular among mechanics in general and among horse-shoers in particular, as the horse-rasps made at the Chelsea File Works are conceded to be superior to anything else in the market. There is certainly no reason why the files and rasps made here should not give the very best of satisfaction, for they are exclusively hand-cut and are made from the finest material obtainable, by skilled workmen. As for prices, they are also uniformly satisfactory, for while Mr. Butts does not pretend to quote equally low rates with the manufacturers of cheap (and comparatively worthless machine-cut files, still he does sell as low as the lowest, quality considered; and the superior efficiency and durability of his goods make them the cheapest to buy in the long run. Employment is given to thirty competent assistants, and all orders are assured immediate and painstaking attention.

William Tubbs, manufacturer of Carts, Drays and Steamboat Trucks, No. 13 Bath Street, Norwich, Conn.— It would never do to omit mention of the enterprise conducted by Mr. William Tubbs in a review of the representative business undertakings of this city, for certainly the enterprise in question is representative in the best sense of the word, it having been in successful operation for more than half a century. Business was begun by Messrs. Cranston & Tubbs in 1837, and the location has been unchanged from the beginning In 1839, the present proprietor assumed sole control and the business has since developed until it has reached its present large proportions. Mr. Tubbs was born in Lisbon, Conn., and has been very prominent in municipal as well as in business affairs. He served four years in the common council and was at one time at the head of the fire department. He was also a delegate to the State Convention of 1856-7. A specialty is made of the manufacture of carts, drays, and steamboat trucks, but carriages and other light vehicles are also made to order at short notice and at moderate rates. The premises utilized comprise two shops, each of which measures about 65 × 20 feet. Jobbing is given prompt and painstaking attention, and carriage repairing and painting will be done in first-class style at short notice, as will also horseshoeing and blacksmithing in general. Horse owners and others are very well acquainted with the advantages to be derived from placing their orders at an establishment where they will be assured immediate and skillful attention, and it is therefore natural that Mr. Tubbs should do a large and steady business.

E. W. Yerrington, wholesale and retail dealer in Paper Hangings, Curtains and Borders, Carpeting, Oil Cloths, Rugs, Mats, etc. Sole agent for Chickering & Sons' Pianos, and Loring & Blake's Cabinet Organs, 130 Main Street, Norwich, Conn.—It is very difficult to compress a comprehensive notice of the enterprise conducted by Mr. E. W. Yerrington within our necessarily narrow limits, for the simple reason that that gentleman carries on so large and varied a business that it is practically equivalent to the enterprise conducted by several ordinary firms. Mr. Yerrington was born in Norwich and is very widely known, not only in business circles but also among gentlemen sportsmen, for he is one of the most famous trap shots in the State. He founded his present business in 1862, and it has developed very extensively in every department. A wholesale and retail trade is carried on in paper hangings, curtains and borders, carpeting, oil cloths and other floor coverings, and a large business is also done in pianos, organs, etc. The premises occupied are located at No. 130 Main street, and have been utilized by Mr. Yerrington for more than a score of years. The first floor is fitted up in an elegant and tasteful manner, and will compare favorably in every respect with some of the most pretentious New York establishments. This floor is devoted expressly to the sale of wall papers, curtains and interior decorations, and contains a stock which comprises the latest fashionable novelties, as well as a full line of department. The second floor is utilized for the accommodation of a large and costly stock of pianos and organs, all the leading makes being handled, and from twenty-five to thirty pianos being carried in stock at a time. Mr. Yerrington is sole agent for Chickering & Sons pianos, and Loring & Blake's cabinet organs, and is prepared to sell or to rent pianos and organs on the most favorable terms, all goods being warranted as represented. The third floor contains a magnificent assortment of carpetings and other floor coverings, comprising the latest patterns and the productions of the most reputable makers. Goods are cheerfully shown at any time, and no house is in a position to quote lower prices on articles of equal merit.

Geo. S. Smith, Franklin Steam Mills. Sole manufacturer of Palmer's Celebrated Dandelion Coffee, 11 and 13 Commerce Street, Norwich, Conn.— No name among those associated with the early history of this country is more worthy of honor than that of Franklin, and no enterprise of a similar character is more deserving of the most favorable mention that can be given it than that carried on under the style of the "Franklin Steam Mills," for since this undertaking was founded more than forty years ago, it has been so managed as to have gained the entire confidence of consumers and the trade. Operations were begun in 1846, by Mr. C. J. Palmer, who finally gave place to Mr. John Willard, he being succeeded by the present proof East Lyme Conn., but has been in active business life in this city for more than a score of years. Those familiar with the standing of the Franklin Steam Mills previous to the time Mr. Smith assumed control, will need no more convincing proof of his ability and integrity than that contained in the fact that he has not only maintained its reputation but has materially added to it while developing the business in every department. The mills are located at Nos. 11 and 13 Commerce street, and comprise four floors of the dimensions of 90 × 30 feet each. Among the leading commodities handled may be mentioned green, roasted, and ground coffees, spices, mustard, and cream tartar, together with a full line of fine teas, and we must by no means omit mention of Palmer's celebrated dandelion coffee, for Mr. Smith makes a specialty of this highly popular preparation of which he is sole manufacturer. An exclusively wholesale business is done, no goods being sold at retail under any circumstances, and Mr. Smith is prepared not only to quote bottom prices but to guarantee the quality of the various goods he handles, for he roasts the coffees and grinds his own spices, etc. A large force of assistants is employed and the very heaviest orders can be promptly and satisfactorily filled.

Dime Savings Bank, Norwich, Conn.—It is but fair to presume that every savings bank in this State is in a perfectly solvent condition and is worthy of all confidence, for those having charge of Connecticut savings banks are men of experience, ability and integrity, and these institutions are also under strict State supervision, their managers being legally forbidden to invest in " wild-cat " securities of any kind. But while all may be almost equally reliable, it by no means follows that all are equally popular, for, unfortunately, some are conducted on such cast-iron principles that depositors are kept at arm's-length, as it were, and are obliged to go through all sorts of formalities before transacting whatever business they may desire to carry out. Some formalities are of course necessary and these are not at all objectionable, but the public are quick to appreciate the difference between red tape and judicious business safeguards, and it is largely owing to this quickness of appreciation that the Dime Savings Bank has so rapidly gained in popularity and influence since beginning operations about a score of years ago. Its policy of receiving the smallest sums of money (from a dime upwards) is of itself enough to commend it to wage-earners, and in every detail of its management is exhibited the same liberal and intelligent desire to cater to the wants of the people The bank was organized in 1869 and its steady growth in public confidence since that date is eloquently shown by the following figures:

DEPOSITS ON MAY 1.

Year 1870, $39,454 78; 1871, $172,269.52; 1872, $376,-624.45; 1873, $654,179 73; 1874, $925,728.77; 1875, $957,-484.16; 1876, $1,128,362.37; 1877, $1,225,233.31; 1878, $1,119,463 15; 1879, $1,032,436 84; 1880, $1,035,014.76; 1881, $1,145,868 96; 1882, $1,219,843.06; 1883, $1,260,139,-70; 1884, $1,284,205.50; 1885, $1,277,549 83; 1886, $1,268,-880.71; 1887, $1,357,331 38; 1888, $1,393,047.12; 1889, $1,459,495.77.

As liberal a rate of interest is allowed on deposits as the conditions of the market will permit, and the fact that the total surplus for protection of depositors amounts to about $70,000, while the deposits are upwards of about one and one-half million of dollars, shows that the management is as conservative as it is energetic. The officers and directors are widely-known business men, as will be plainly seen from a perusal of the following list:

President, E. R. Thompson.

Vice-presidents, Hugh H. Osgood, Willis R. Austin and J. Hunt Smith.

Secretary and treasurer, Frank L. Woodard. .

Attorney, Gardiner Greene, Jr.

Directors, Wm. C. Osgood, F. J. Leavens, W. R. Burnham, C. D. Browning, Gardiner Greene, Jr., E. G. Bidwell, Geo. C. Raymond, Nicholas Tarrant, I. W. Carpenter and Frank L. Woodard.

N. S. Gilbert & Sons, jobbers and retailers of Furniture, Carpets, Wall Papers, Window Shades, Drapery Curtains, Rugs and Mats, 137 and 141 Main Street, Norwich, Conn. Furniture Factory, Cor. Chestnut and Willow Streets.—It is a very common mistake to assume that because a firm has the reputation of handling strictly reliable goods, it must necessarily quote high prices. An examination of the extensive assortment of house furnishing goods shown by this firm, will convince the intelligent purchaser that ample returns are made for each investment, and that the firm possess unequaled facilities for producing and handling each line they represent. The senior member of the firm attends in person to the furniture factory, cor. Chestnut and Willow streets, where all special orders of furniture are made. Prior to the late war, the factory manufactured for the Southern trade, but since that time, the present stores, 137 and 139 Main street, have received the full product. Here everything in the way of furniture can be found. Chamber sets of mahogany, cherry, antique oak, ash, walnut, etc., are shown in great variety. Also, dining room and library furniture of the latest and most approved styles. The parlor sets with their rich coverings in silks and plushes also demand their share of admiration. The prices for these goods average about *one third* of those of twenty years ago, and show astonishing progress in manner of production and novelty of style. The carpet warerooms are replete with beautiful fabrics, and this stock is hardly equalled in the State. Moquettes, axminsters, velvets, brussels, ingrains, rugs and mats, all invite the housekeeper and delight the ladies. Practical carpet layers are always in attendance, insuring the best quality of work in fitting and laying carpets with borders. The prices are below those of New York and Boston, for the same goods, and have induced a large trade from the surrounding towns to center with N. S. Gilbert & Sons. To make their stock most complete, the firm some three years ago, added a complete stock of wall papers, so that they can execute orders for furnishing a room entirely. They decorate the walls, carpet the floors and upholster the furniture in harmonizing colors and tints, giving the benefit of their study and experience to assist the purchaser. Their warerooms occupy three spacious floors, and the opportunities for the display and inspection of the mammoth stock carried are all that could be desired. Employment is given to forty assistants, and both a wholesale and retail business is done, orders being at all times assured immediate and painstaking attention. Callers are waited upon promptly and politely, and a visit to this representative store is sure to prove a pleasant experience.

George F. Bard, Plumber, Steam and Gas Fitter, Brass Founder and Coppersmith ; dealer in Wrought Iron Pipe, Fittings, Valves, Engineers' Supplies, etc. No. 24 Ferry Street. Norwich, Conn.—It is just about a score of years since Mr. Geo. F. Bard became identified with his present business, for he engaged in it in 1870 as a member of the firm of Pierce & Bard, this concern succeeding Mr. Geo. Pierce who had had control since 1865, the enterprise having been inaugurated in 1829 by Messrs. Pierce & Roberts. Mr. Bard was born in Boston, and doubtless owes much of the success he has won to his intimate knowledge of every detail of his business and his habit of giving it close personal supervision. The premises made use of are very spacious and they have need to be, for Mr. Bard carries on several distinct lines of business ; being a plumber, steam and gas fitter; a brass founder and coppersmith; and a dealer in engineers' supplies, wrought iron pipe, fittings valves, etc. The foundry is built of brick, is 100 × 70 feet in dimensions, and is fitted up with the most improved facilities, enabling the best of work to be done and the most extensive orders to be filled at short notice. Extensive warehouses are also utilized, and a varied and valuable stock is constantly carried. Employment is given to twenty five assistants and orders for plumbing, steam and gas fitting are assured immediate and painstaking attention. Moderate charges are made and no better work is done by any house in this city.

John B. Shaw, manufacturer of Fine Harness, and dealer in Trunks, Traveling Bags, Valises, Blankets, Mats, Whips, Saddles, Carriage Robes, etc., 90 Main Street, Franklin Square, Norwich.— We venture to assert that there are few experienced horsemen in Norwich and vicinity who are unacquainted with the establishment conducted by Mr. John B. Shaw at No. 90 Main street, for this gentleman is an extensive manufacturer of and dealer in fine harness, and also handles trunks, travelling bags, valises, blankets, mats, whips, saddles, carriage robes, etc. He has carried on his present business for more than forty years, and his productions have long been accepted as the standard by those familiar with them and competent to appreciate honest stock and skillful and conscientious workmanship. Mr. Shaw is very widely known personally in Norwich, having served several terms on the city council as well as being prominent in business circles. His establishment occupies premises of the dimensions of 75×25 feet, and contains a handsome and varied stock which bears evidence of careful selection in every detail. Employment is afforded to four efficient assistants, and callers are sure of receiving prompt and polite attention, while custom work and repairing will be done at the shortest possible notice and at prices as low as is consistent with the use of suitable material and the employment of skilled labor.

C. E. Dudley, dealer in Fresh and Salt Meats, 127 West Main Street, Norwich, Conn.—The business conducted by Mr. C. E. Dudley at No. 127 West Main street was founded not far from forty years ago, operations having been begun by Mr. C. J. Winters in 1853. Mr. E. A. Dudley, father of the present proprietor, assumed control of the enterprise in 1878, and gave place to his son in the early part of 1887. Mr. C. E. Dudley was born in Massachusetts, but has become thoroughly identified with Norwich business interests and ranks with the most enterprising and successful of our city merchants. He deals very extensively in fresh and salt meats of all kinds and carries a stock which in point of size, completeness and variety has few rivals in this section of the State among the assortments offered by retail dealers. It is this variety which has much to do with the general popularity of the enterprise, for all classes of customers can here find goods suited to their tastes and purses, and it is easy to see that Mr. Dudley caters with equal care to rich and poor; his policy being to ensure uniform satisfaction and uniform courtesy to large and small buyers. Employment is given to four competent and polite assistants, and as several teams are utilized all orders can be accurately delivered at the shortest possible notice.

A. Francis & Co., dealers in Domestic Dry Goods, Yankee Notions, Crockery, Groceries and Provisions, Corner Main and Thames Streets, West Side, Norwich, Conn.—The establishment conducted by Messrs. A. Francis & Co., at the corner of Main and Thames streets, West Side, probably approaches as near to being a regular old-fashioned "country store" as any place of business in Norwich, for it combines the noteworthy characteristics of such a store with the enterprise and energy of a city establishment. City people are apt to smile good naturedly at the immense variety of widely diverse articles offered at a country store, and yet they appreciate the convenience of being able to buy "everything at once," while they are amused and sometimes annoyed at the length of time it takes to get an order filled. Messrs. A. Francis & Co. are prepared to furnish about anything in the line of domestic dry goods, Yankee notions, crockery, groceries and provisions; and to serve customers as promptly and politely as though a specialty was made of the handling of any one of the lines of goods we have mentioned. Many of our readers do not need to be told this, for the enterprise in question has been carried on for many years, and the methods of the firm are well and favorably known to a large portion of the community. Operations were begun by Mr. A. Francis, in 1853, and the present firm-name was adopted in 1874, the partners being Messrs. A. and J. P. Francis; the former a native of Stafford, and the latter of this city. Mr. A. Francis served four years in the common council, and both members of the firm are so well known as not to call for further personal mention. Every detail of the business is given careful supervision and the goods, the prices, and the service are uniformly and equally satisfactory.

A. T. Davis, dealer in New and Second hand House-Furnishing Goods, sold on Commission, 11 Thames Street, Norwich.—There are many careful housekeepers to be found in Norwich and vicinity, and not a few of them have discovered that the establishment conducted by Mr. A. T. Davis at No. 11 Thames street, is a most excellent one to visit when anything in the shape of crockery ware or other house furnishing goods is wanted, new or second-hand. This business was founded by Mr. Davis about the year 1875, and during the time since elapsed it has steadily and largely developed. The proprietor is thoroughly familiar with every detail of the trade, and in fact gives it such close and constant personal attention that the high degree of success attained is certainly thoroughly well deserved. An extensive commission business is carried on, the value of the goods annually disposed of reaching a very high figure. The premises made use of are 50 × 40 feet in dimensions, and afford ample opportunity for the carrying of a heavy stock and the displaying of it to excellent advantage. A full selection of staple styles is always on hand to choose from, embracing furniture, carpets, oil-cloths, crockery, etc., together with a complete assortment of the latest fashionable novelties, so that all tastes as well as all purses can be easily suited.

F. E. Dowe, Fancy Dry Goods and Novelties; Specialties : Art Embroidery Materials of every description, Cotton Underwear, Infants' Furnishings, Hosiery, Kid Gloves, Laces, Ribbons, Trimmings ; 157 Main and 19 Shetucket Streets, Norwich, Conn. Summer branch, "The Bazaar," Watch Hill, R. I.—Notwithstanding the high average character of the many mercantile establishments located in Norwich and vicinity, it is obvious that here as elsewhere there must be certain houses in each line of trade which excel all others in the handling of given specialties, and it is an open secret that at the establishment conducted by Mr. F. E. Dowe, at No. 157 Main street and 19 Shetucket street, unequaled inducements are offered to purchasers of art embroidery materials of every description, cotton underwear, infants' furnishings, hosiery, kid gloves, laces, ribbons and trimmings. Mr. Dowe certainly ought to be able to offer exceptional advantages to buyers of these goods or of any other articles of which he makes specialties, for he has had long and varied experience in his present line of business (having founded the enterprise under consideration in 1872) and enjoys such favorable relations with producers and wholesalers as to enable him to quote positively bottom prices on positively dependable goods. He is a native of Springfield, Mass., and has long ranked among our representative Norwich merchants. The store utilized by him is shaped like an "L" and measures 20×50×40 feet, opportunity being given for the carrying of a very heavy and varied stock, and for the displaying of it to excellent advantage. Fancy art goods and novelties, in almost endless variety are at hand to select from, and the employment of six competent assistants assures prompt and polite attention to every customer. Mr. Dowe is the owner of the famous "Bazaar" at Watch Hill, R. I., which is very largely patronized during the summer months and has done much to add to its proprietor's reputation.

Robert Brown, Steam and Gas Fitter and Plumber, Pequot Building, Central Wharf, Norwich, Conn.— "Modern conveniences" would certainly not willingly be dispensed with, and their advantages far outweigh their disadvantages, but nevertheless it is undoubtedly a fact that the plumbing arrangements of a house must be properly put in, duly cared for and kept in perfect repair or they are apt to breed sickness, especially in thickly-settled communities. Everything depends upon having the plumbing work of a house properly done to begin with, for alterations are often difficult and expensive to make and even when made the result is liable to be less satisfactory than would have been the case had the work been originally done correctly. Among those engaged in the plumbing business in this vicinity, none is better known than Mr. Robert Brown, for this gentleman began operations over a score of years ago (in 1868) and has for a long time held a leading position in his branch of industry. Mr. Brown is a native of South Kingston, R. I., and has held many public offices, having been connected with the city council for some fourteen years, and having served as alderman, as water commissioner and as chairman of the board of education. He deals very extensively in plumbing supplies, both at wholesale and retail, and carries a very heavy stock, three floors being utilized, each measuring fifty feet square; the premises being located on Central wharf, in the Pequot Building. Employment is given to sixteen competent assistants, and gas-fitting, steam fitting, plumbing, etc., will be done in a superior manner at very short notice and at a moderate charge. Mr. Brown did the plumbing work for a large proportion of the more important buildings in this section, and is prepared to guarantee satisfaction to the most critical.

D. W. Grant, dealer in Groceries and Provisions, Teas, Coffees, Spices, Canned Goods, Cigars, Tobacco, etc., 169 West Main street, Norwich, Conn.—It is the simple truth to say that the average grocery and provision store in Norwich will compare favorably with the average establishment of the kind in any other city in New England, and therefore when we assert that the store conducted by Mr. D. W. Grant, at No. 169 West Main street, is superior to the average in more respects than one, it is obvious that we are giving it high praise. And yet we are confident that such of our readers as are qualified to judge will admit that it is well deserved. Mr. Grant carries a heavy and varied stock of choice groceries and provisions, teas, coffees, spices, canned goods, cigars, tobacco, etc., and guarantees each and every article he sells to prove just as represented, and quotes the lowest market rates. Add to these recommendations the fact that orders are promptly and accurately filled, and it must be confessed that the showing is a strong one. The more closely it is investigated, the more fully it will be found to be warranted by the facts, and so thoroughly convinced are we of this that we have no hesitation in guaranteeing complete satisfaction to all reasonable people who may favor Mr. Grant with their custom. He is a native of Freeport, Maine, and established his present business in 1886. Close personal attention is given to every detail, and no trouble is spared to maintain the high reputation already won.

GEORGE E. PITCHER.

CIVIL ENGINEER,

SURVEYOR AND

CONTRACTOR,

12 SHETUCKET ST.,   NORWICH, CONN.

Theron E. Brown, Hack, Livery, Boarding and Feed Stable ; Attendance on Funerals, Weddings and Parties at reasonable prices ; Railroad Avenue, opposite Norwich & Worcester Passenger Depot, Norwich, Conn.— The establishment located on Railroad avenue, near the Norwich & Worcester Depot and owned by Mr. T. E. Brown, is a public benefit and is worthy of prominent and favorable mention ; first, because a good team may be hired here at moderate expense, second, because horses may be put to board here in the full assurance that they will have comfortable quarters, good food and careful and skillful attention, and third, because horses may be bought here without paying double their true value—which is more than can be said of some "sale stables" which could be mentioned. Now it is obvious that such an enterprise as this, managed as this is, is a great accommodation to the public and we are very glad to be able to say that the public appreciate this fact and show their appreciation by liberally patronizing the establishment in question. Mr. Brown was born in Colchester, Conn., and founded his present business in 1881. He employs two competent assistants, but makes it a point to give careful personal attention to affairs, thus ensuring prompt, courteous and dependable service. Teams will be furnished at very short notice and at prices that are really exceptionally low considering the nature of the accommodations provided.

Daniel J. Brown, dealer in Second-hand Machinery. Guns and Locks repaired ; Stocks bent to any desired shape ; Second-hand Guns bought and sold ; Keys fitted. 111 Water Street, Norwich, Conn.—It is one thing to buy a good gun and another to get a gun repaired in first class style, and all who have had experience will agree that the latter is the harder of the two to accomplish For this reason, such of our readers as have sporting tastes will thank us for calling to their attention the facilities possessed by Mr. Daniel J. Brown for the repairing of guns and fire-arms in general, for he makes a specialty of such work and has the skill and the tools to attain results that are bound to suit the most critical. Stocks will be bent to any desired drop, and all orders are assured prompt and careful attention. Mr. Brown buys and sells second-hand guns and generally has some excellent weapons on hand which may be bought for comparatively little money. Second hand machinery is also dealt in to a considerable extent, and locksmithing in all its branches is carried on, locks being repaired and keys fitted at very short notice and at uniformly moderate rates. Mr. Brown gives personal attention to the various details of his business and has established an enviable reputation for punctuality and skill in the filling of orders. He is a native of Hartford, and founded his present business in 1882. Mr. Brown also buys and sells antique fire arms, powder horns, Indian relics, swords, daggers, and antiquities of this description. He has also a breech loading, flint-lock gun made at Harper's Ferry in 1832 ; these are very rare at the present time.

Norwich Paper Box Company, manufacturers of Paper Boxes, S. E. Bliven, proprietor, 101 Broadway, Norwich, Conn. It is difficult to see how paper boxes could be dispensed with nowadays, for they are used for such a great variety of purposes and have proved of such great convenience that the public would strongly resent any attempt to go back to the conditions present at the time such boxes were introduced The manufacture of paper boxes has become a great and growing industry, and among the many concerns engaged in it the Norwich Paper Box Company should be given a prominent position, for since operations were begun in 1885 the company has built up an enviable reputation for the uniform excellence of its goods and the promptness and accuracy shown in the filling of orders. The premises utilized are located at No. 101 Broadway and comprise two floors of the dimensions of 85x60 feet. The factory is equipped with improved machinery, and all sorts of paper boxes are made, large and small orders being given equally careful attention. Employment is given to twelve competent assistants, and the company is in a position to meet all honorable competition, quoting the lowest market rates on goods of standard quality. The proprietor of this business is Mr. S. E. Bliven, who was born in Windham, Conn., and gives close personal attention to the filling of every order.

William Blackburn, Blacksmithing, 15 Myer's Alley, Norwich, Conn.—The introduction of machinery has worked radical changes in every line of mechanical business, but probably blacksmithing has been affected least of all, for although nowadays a man may call himself a machinist and yet know little more about the trade than how to adjust a lathe or a milling machine, and to see that it does its work properly ; if he is to be a blacksmith he must be able to use hand tools to some advantage, and in short must be a mechanic and not merely a machine tender. There is more difference in blacksmiths than in machinists for the simple reason that under existing conditions more skill is required in the former trade and more opportunity given for a man to "show what he is made of" from a mechanical point of view. We take pleasure in calling favorable attention to the shop of William Blackburn, located at No. 15 Myer's alley, for not only is this very completely fitted up with improved facilities of various kinds, but the work turned out will bear the severest examination, being strictly first-class and combining strength, neatness, and durability. Sufficient assistance is employed to assure the prompt filling of all orders, and a great variety of work is done, including horse shoeing, general iron and steel jobbing, the repairing of springs, and, in short, blacksmithing and carriage work in all its branches, including wood-work also. Moderate charges are made in every instance and we are glad to say that the extent and constant growth of the business show that the liberal methods of Mr. William Blackburn are appreciated.

Albert L. Potter & Co., Coal and Domestic Lumber, Chestnut, Oak and Hickory Wood; also Piling, Fence Posts and Ship Timber; 18 Broadway, Norwich, Conn.—The firm of Albert L. Potter & Co. do both a wholesale and retail business, ard rank with the leading houses in their line in Eastern Connecticut. The undertaking carried on by them was founded in 1868, by Mr. A. R. Clark, and was continued in 1883 by Messrs. Potter & Harris, the present firm name being adopted in 1887. The existing concern is made up of Messrs. Albert L., and Frank Potter, both of whom are natives of Voluntown, Conn. Spacious premises are utilized at No. 18 Broadway, the plant in use comprising two mills, large storage sheds for lumber, etc., and coal bins having a capacity of 3000 tons. The firm deal very largely in coal, and enjoy an extensive family trade, as they handle all the more popular brands for household consumption, and quote bottom rates at all times, besides being remarkably prompt and accurate in the delivery of orders. Chestnut, oak and hickory wood are also extensively dealt in and so is domestic lumber, together with piling, fence posts and ship timber. The mills are equipped with the very latest improved machinery, including a Hendley Automatic Steam Engine, and their combined capacity approximates 15,000 feet per day. Employment is given to twenty assistants and every order, large or small, is sure of receiving prompt and careful attention.

Welcome A. Smith, wholesale and retail dealer in Staple and Fancy Groceries, 137 Main Street, and 156 Water Street, Norwich, Conn.—There is no risk taken in asserting that the enterprise conducted by Mr. Welcome A. Smith is at least as well known an undertaking of its kind as the city of Norwich can show, for no one will be likely to dispute a statement so thoroughly in accordance with the facts. Business was begun in 1868, by Messrs. Smith Brothers, the firm name afterward becoming Smith

& Reynolds, then Smith & Beckwith, and finally in 1884, Welcome A. Smith. The proprietor is a native of Griswold, Ct., and is very widely known both in business and in social circles throughout this vicinity. He is a wholesale and retail dealer in staple and fancy groceries, and occupies spacious premises at 137 Main street, and 156 Water street, carrying a very heavy and valuable stock, and being prepared to fill the most extensive orders without delay. Employment is given to seven assistants, and callers are assured prompt and courteous attention—a fact which explains to some extent at least the general popularity of the store among all classes of people, for no discrimination is made between large and small buyers as regards the courtesy extended. Mr. Smith quotes the lowest market rates on the many goods he handles, and the assurance that you are getting just what you pay for is another potent factor in the steady increase of his trade.

S. A. Bailey, dealer in Fresh and Salt Meats, Poultry, Beef Tongues, Hams, Vegetables and Canned Goods, 161 Franklin Street, Norwich, Conn.—We do not admit the soundness of all the arguments which are presented to show the advantage gained by dealing with those making a specialty of the handling of certain lines of goods, but still it is doubtless true that, other things being equal, a man who deals in nothing but meats and vegetables should be able to offer greater inducements than one who considers the handling of these products as but a comparatively small portion of his business. As a practical illustration of the nature and magnitude of these inducements, let us call the attention of our readers to the advantages offered by Mr. S. A. Bailey, doing business at No. 161 Franklin street, for he makes a specialty of dealing in fresh and salt meats, poultry, beef tongues, hams, vegetables and canned goods, and certainly supplies thoroughly first-class articles at the very lowest market rates. Mr. Bailey first became associated with his present enterprise as a member of the firm of T. M. Frazier & Co., who began operations in 1885, and were succeeded by the present owner two years later. He has greatly developed the business since assuming sole control. Orders will be called for and goods delivered in any part of the city, and sufficient assistance is employed to ensure prompt and painstaking attention to every caller.

Timothy Kelly, dealer in Groceries, Provisions, Boots, Shoes and Rubbers, Crockery, Glass, Wood and Willow Ware, 197 North Main Street, Norwich, Conn.—Of course in the compilation of a book of this kind it is not always easy to determine the proper degree of prominence to give the various business enterprises of which mention is made, but this difficulty is not present in all classes by any means, as there are certain undertakings the representative character of which is so apparent as to be obvious, making their title to a leading position in any review of the section's business houses clear beyond dispute. In this class must be placed the establishment, carried on by Timothy Kelly, at 197 North Main St., for the many years that his undertaking has been conducted, and the unsurpassed reputation for fair dealing and enterprise enjoyed by the manager combine to make it representative in the full sense of the word. The enterprise in question was founded in 1870 under the firm name of Kelly & Brother and so continued until 1873, when Mr. Timothy Kelly assumed entire proprietorship. The premises occupied comprise a store 40×40 feet in dimensions, together with a storehouse of two stories each 40×40 feet in size, and the stock on hand is sufficiently large to test the capacity of even this amount of space, for it is exceptionally complete in every department and comprises groceries, provisions, boots, shoes and rubbers, crockery glass, wood and willow ware, grain, flour, feed, etc. Employment is given to four efficient assistants, and customers are promptly served, while the magnitude and character of the trade are enough to prove that the proprietor handles only reliable goods and quotes low prices in every department.

Seth L. Peck, wholesale and retail dealer in Masons' Building Materials and Stone Work of all kinds, Central Wharf, Norwich, Conn.—Such an important trade centre as Norwich would naturally be a depot for the reception and distribution of building materials, etc., and as a matter of fact this has long been a very important item in our local wholesale and retail trade. The leading dealer in masons' building materials, etc., in this vicinity is Mr. Seth L. Peck, and the business conducted by him is of very early origin, having been founded by Mr. Geo. E. Hebard nearly half a century ago, or in 1845. The present proprietor was born in Lyme, Conn., and assumed control of the enterprise in 1871. He utilizes very spacious premises on Central Wharf, and carries an extremely heavy, varied and costly stock, comprising masons' building materials, and stone work of all kinds. The extent and variety of this assortment are not to be appreciated without personal inspection, but it will aid our readers in getting an idea of its completeness when we say it includes Philadelphia front brick, white front brick, eastern lime, Glen Falls' and St. Albans' lime, Rosendale and Portland Roman cement, plaster, hair, fire brick, fire clay, beach sand, mortar ready mixed, blue stone flagging, curbing, granite and brown stone, cut and in rough, drain and sewer pipe of all kinds, marble and marbleized slate mantels, house sheathing papers of every description, and moth proof carpet felts. Mr. Peck is prepared to furnish any or all of these commodities in quantities to suit at short notice, and to quote positively bottom prices on both large and small orders.

Wm. L. Patton & Co., Bankers and Brokers, 6 Wall Street, New York. Shetucket Street. Norwich, Conn.— The New York firm of William L. Patton & Co. is very widely and favorably known here in Connecticut for this concern has branch houses in New London, Hartford and this city and has transacted a very large amount of business for local investors to the entire satisfaction of every reasonable patron. The firm have unsurpassed facilities for obtaining the earliest quotations from the great centres of trade, and those who wish to invest in petroleum, corn, wheat or other staples, or in stocks or bonds cannot possibly do so to better advantage elsewhere. The Norwich office was opened in 1883 and is under the charge of Mr. J. E. McGarry, who is a native of New London and who can need no introduction to many of our readers for he is prominent in business and social circles and is very widely known. Mr. McGarry has made the Norwich branch as important and popular an office as the firm maintain, and it is receiving a constantly increasing patronage as the advantages offered become more generally known. The premises utilized are located at No. 14 Shetucket street, and are very completely fitted up, the comfort and convenience of patrons being carefully provided for.

Frank B. Gay, dealer in Fine Groceries, Canned Goods and Fruits, No. 2 Cliff Street, Norwich, Conn.—One's first impression on examining the stock carried by Mr. Frank B. Gay at No. 2 Cliff street, is that it is decidedly superior to the average in quality and will compare favorably in point of size, and this impression will be confirmed by more extended investigation for Mr. Gay takes pains to handle goods that will suit the most fastidious, and to offer a sufficient variety to enable all tastes to be suited and all orders to be filled without delay. He is a native of Preston, and has carried on his present business since 1885. The premises utilized have an area of about 1500 square feet, and afford excellent opportunity for the accommodation of a complete assortment of staple and fancy groceries, table condiments, canned goods, fruits, etc., the stock being so arranged as to aid materially in the prompt and accurate filling of orders. Mr. Gay gives close personal attention to the enterprise, but employs two competent assistants and neglects no means to fully deserve the exceptional popularity his establishment has won. This popularity is of course due to the promptness and courtesy of the service to a great extent, but even more to the fact that every article will prove precisely as represented.

W. W. Ives, Nickle and Silver Plater, manufacturer of Window Display Frames for Gents' Furnishing, Boot and Shoe, Hat, Millinery and Dry Goods Stores, Special Fixtures made to order, 11 Myers Alley, Norwich, Conn.—It pays to display goods attractively, and no stronger proof of this is needed than the fact that the leading dry goods houses, etc., employ men at high salaries, whose sole duty is to design and superintend the window display. It is all very well to say that honest goods will sell on their merits; that "good wine needs no bush," and that a reputation for giving full value for money received is all that is necessary in order to do a profitable business; but experience proves that, other things being equal, he whose stock is most attractively shown will get the bulk and also the cream of the patronage. In calling attention to the window display frames made by Mr. W. W. Ives, we are not recommending new and untried articles, for these have been on the market for some years and have given entire satisfaction wherever used. They are ingeniously and handsomely designed; solidly constructed from the best of material; are effective, durable and reasonable in price; and are especially adapted to the use of those dealing in boots and shoes, gents' furnishings, hats and caps, millinery or dry goods. Special fixtures will be made to order at moderate prices, and there is no retailer but what can make profitable use of Mr. Ives' productions. The standard styles made by him are the " Nonpareil" and the " Champion " ; the former being fitted with his new " Eureka" rest, which holds the shoe or other article so firmly that it cannot be shaken off by the slamming of doors or any other jar, while at the same time it does not mar the article nor hide its outlines. The " Nonpareil" stand with " Eureka" rest for the display of single articles is a very popular style, as is also the " Nonpareil" swing bracket with " Eureka" rest. All these goods, with numerous other styles, are made from the best of material, are heavily nickel plated and will not rust under any circumstances, no iron entering into their construction. Mr. Ives is a native of New Haven, and gives careful attention to every order. He maintains a thoroughly equipped shop at No. 11 Myers alley, and is prepared to fill all orders at short notice, nickel plating and brass finishing being done in a superior manner at a moderate charge. He also plates novelties of all kinds for other manufacturers.

Thomas E. Casey, dealer in Fresh and Salt Meats, Beef, Pork, Mutton, Lamb, Veal, Poultry, etc., 471 North Main Street, Greeneville, Conn.—Among the recently established houses in Greeneville that carry a superior grade of fresh and salt meats, that conducted by Thomas E. Casey, located at No. 471 North Main street, deserves special mention. This house was established in 1888 by its present proprietor, who has by energy and perseverance, attained the position he now occupies among the business men of Greeneville. The business premises occupied by him are 40 × 18 feet in dimensions, and are admirably arranged for his trade, having all necessary facilities for carrying on the business. Courteous and obliging assistants are constantly employed, while the stock embraces all kinds of fresh and salt meats, a specialty being made of beef, pork, mutton, lamb, veal, poultry, etc., Mr. Casey's facilities for handling choice goods being unsurpassed in this vicinity. He is an energetic gentleman of long experience in his business, to which he devotes his close personal attention, thus insuring perfect satisfaction in all respects to his numerous patrons. Mr. Casey is a native of Norwich, and well deserves the success he has attained.

Tompkins & Murphy, dealers in Hardware, Stoves, Tin and Wooden Ware; Tin Roofing, Roof Painting, Plumbing and Factory Work; all kinds of Repairs for Stoves, Ranges and Furnaces; Telephone orders to Bisket & Meech; No. 26 Sixth Street, Greeneville, Conn.—Of late years there have been great improvements in certain lines of manufacture, and in no industry has much greater progress been made than in that relating to the production of stoves and ranges. Some of the parlor stoves now on the market combine beauty and efficiency to a remarkable degree, but there are others which are of but little use except for purely ornamental purposes, for their designers in attaining beauty of form and decoration, seriously injured the heating qualities. However, there is no need of purchasing a stove defective in any respect, and the best way to avoid doing so is to buy of such dealers as Messrs. Tompkins & Murphy, for they have had sufficient experience to be thoroughly familiar with the leading styles of heating and cooking stoves and they handle none which they have reasons to believe will not give satisfaction. This firm is made up of Messrs. J. F. Tompkins and C. O. Murphy. The former began operations in 1887, and the present firm in 1888. The premises utilized by them are located at No. 26 Sixth street, a large stock of hardware, stoves, tin and wooden ware is constantly carried. The lowest market rates are quoted, and tin roofing, roof painting, plumbing, and factory work, also all kinds of repairs for stoves, ranges, and furnaces are done in the most workmanlike manner at very short notice. Employment is given to four competent and reliable workmen, and all orders by telephone, or otherwise delivered, will receive prompt and satisfactory attention.

Pitcher & Maine, dealers in Dry Goods, Groceries, Boots, Shoes, Crockery, etc., 428½ to 434 North Main Street, Norwich, Conn.—There is a certain air about a popular and well-patronized establishment of any kind that is easily distinguished by a careful observer, and although it would often be difficult to define just what is meant by an " air of prosperity," still it is impossible to mistake such an appearance after once becoming familiar with it. If any of our readers wish an example of what we mean let them visit the establishment now conducted by Messrs. Pitcher & Maine, and they will find one of the most popular stores in this section. This establishment was founded in 1859. Messrs. A. H., and H. A Pitcher assumed control; the present firm of Pitcher & Maine was formed in 1888. The premises occupied are 40 × 60 feet in dimensions and are located on North Main street, from Nos. 428½ to 434, and afford opportunity for the display of one of the most varied and desirable assortments of dry goods, groceries, boots, shoes, crockery, etc., in Norwich. Employment is given to three competent and polite assistants, and in every department of the store the same scrupulous attention to details is noticeable, the result that customers are always assured prompt and courteous attention, and that the goods offered are both fashionable in style, and low in price, the groceries being fresh and desirable. Messrs. Pitcher & Maine are fully aware that close personal supervision is essential to the maintenance of the admirable system in force in their establishment and may be depended upon in the future as in the past to give their best efforts toward assuring satisfaction to every customer. No misrepresentation is allowed, and prices are made as low as possible.

American House, A. L. Clark, Proprietor, Norwich, Conn.—The American House may properly be called one of the "institutions" of Norwich, for this hotel has been in existence so many years and has been so excellently managed from the start that it is well and favorably known to all whom business or pleasure call frequently to the city. We say "has been" so excellently managed, but by this we do not mean to convey the idea that such management is a thing of the past, and indeed such a judgment would be absurd on the face of it, for the present proprietor, Mr. A. L. Clark, has been in charge a full quarter of a century, having become identified with the enterprise in 1864. He is a native of Oneida County, New York, and there is probably not a hotel man in Connecticut more widely known and highly esteemed. Without making any lavish professions of friendliness he still endeavors to make every guest feel thoroughly at home, and considering his long experience in catering to all classes of people it is hardly necessary to add that he very seldom fails. The American House is a three-story structure, of the dimensions of 50×60 feet, containing thirty guest rooms and being conveniently and pleasantly located on Shetucket street. It is a thoroughly neat and well kept hotel in every respect, and the most fastidious can find no reasonable fault with either the house or its appointments, the beds and other furnishings being modern and comfortable in style, while the service is remarkably efficient, being prompt, intelligent and obliging. The *cuisine* will be found very satisfactory, the table being supplied with an abundance of seasonable food at all times of year. There is a good stable connected with the house, at which single or double teams may be obtained at moderate rates and at very short notice.

Charles L. Baldwin, Hack, Livery, Boarding and Sale Stable, dealer in New and Second-Hand Carriages. Telephone Connection. 127 Franklin Street, Norwich, Conn.—There is of course a market price for horse-hire as there is for flour, for sugar or for any other standard commodity, and those who think to obtain teams at from one third to one-half off the regular rates only deceive themselves, unless of course they are in a position to make special contracts or unless certain circumstances combine to favor them, but still, there is such a thing as paying fancy prices for livery service, and those who do this get no better accommodations than those furnished by Mr. Charles L. Baldwin, who makes it a point to quote the lowest market rates and to fully meet all honorable competition, not only as regards prices but as regards the quality of the turnouts supplied as well. Mr. Baldwin was born in New Haven, and began operations in Norwich in 1871. His stable is located at No. 127 Franklin street, and comprises two floors, measuring 110×40 feet. Employment is given to two assistants, and there are twelve horses and an equal number of carriages available for livery purposes. An extensive hacking, boarding and sale business is also done, fine appearing carriages and experienced drivers being furnished at short notice and special attention being given to boarders and transients. The stable is one of the best ventilated in Connecticut, and with a window for each stall affords ample sunlight and healthy surroundings for the horses. New and second hand carriages are dealt in to a considerable extent, especially low prices being quoted in this department. Mr. Baldwin gives personal attention to clipping, and no better work than that done in this stable is to be had in the city. All orders are assured prompt and painstaking attention, and telephone connection enables them to be sent without trouble from any point in this vicinity.

Small's West Side Store, Nathan Small, Proprietor; Boots, Shoes and Rubbers; Dry Goods and Notions; 3 Thames Street, Small's Block, Norwich, Conn.—The stock to be found at the West Side Shoe Store conducted by Mr. Nathan Small, may be called one of the best "all around " stocks to be seen in this section, for it comprises so great a variety of desirable foot-wear, that men, boys, youths, misses and children, all can find goods within it especially suited to their needs, Mr. Small is well known throughout Norwich, and the fame his new store has already gained as an honestly conducted and liberally managed store, is the legitimate result of his efforts to keep full faith with his customers, and make no announcements not justified by the facts. Mr Small does not allow himself to be undersold by anybody, and therefore those who purchase from him have the satisfaction of knowing that not only are the goods sure to prove as represented, but that they have been bought at the very lowest market rates. The premises utilized are located at No. 3 Thames street, Small's Block, and contain in addition to the fine assortment of boots, shoes and rubbers already mentioned, a carefully selected stock of dry goods and notions of all kinds, the prices of which are guaranteed to suit all. Anyone thinking to purchase any such articles as those dealt in by Mr. Small should give him a call, for his goods are equal to any in the market and are sold at very reasonable figures.

Appley & Prentice, dealers in Choice Family Groceries and Provisions, No. 88 Central Wharf, Norwich, Conn.—Among the many family grocery and provision stores to be found in Norwich and vicinity, that conducted by Messrs. Appley & Prentice is deserving of prominent and favorable mention, not so much on account of any single exceptional inducement which its proprietors offer to the public, as by reason of the " all round " character of the advantages extended, or in other words, Messrs Appley & Prentice don't make a " leader " of any one line of goods, selling them below cost and more than making up on other articles, but they *do* quote the lowest market rates on all the commodities they handle, and they spare no pains to furnish goods that will give the best of satisfaction. This firm began operations in April, 1880, succeeding Mr. O. C. Dimmock who had been in charge since 1880. The present partners are Messrs. Chester Appley and G. C. Prentice, both these gentlemen giving careful personal attention to the filling of orders. The store is located at No. 88 Central Wharf, and measures 45×18 feet, being sufficiently spacious to accommodate a large stock of choice family groceries and provisions. Orders are promptly and accurately filled and every article is sold under a guarantee that it will prove precisely as represented.

Mrs. H. R. Sydleman, dealer in Ladies' Cloaks and Suits, 281 East Main Street, Norwich, Conn.—The establishment conducted by Mrs. H. R. Sydleman at No. 281 East Main street, may be said to be unique of its kind in this vicinity, for there is certainly not a store in this city of precisely similar character. As for the position held by the establishment in question that is very easy to define,— it being generally conceded to have no rival whatever. Mrs. Sydleman began operations about a score of years ago, the business being founded in 1869. She has built up a very extensive and desirable permanent patronage in addition to her large transient trade, and considering her experience, facilities and ability, it is hardly necessary to state that she is prepared to quote the lowest market rates on the goods she handles. The premises utilized are 40 × 20 feet in dimensions and the salesrooms are elegantly and tastefully equipped, while the stock on hand is large, varied and eminently desirable, being made up of the very latest novelties in ladies' cloaks, suits, etc., many successful foreign designs being represented. Employment is afforded to four efficient assistants and orders will be very promptly and carefully filled, every caller being assured immediate and courteous attention.

Brewster Bros., dealers in Choice Groceries, Provisions, Teas, Coffees, Spices, etc., 147 Franklin Street, Norwich, Conn.—There is of course more or less resemblance between all family groceries, and yet each of them has certain characteristics of its own which either commend it or condemn it as the case may be. Take for instance the establishment conducted by Messrs. Brewster Brothers, at No. 147 Franklin street, and we believe it is not at all difficult to account for its popularity, for although other stores may carry equally large stocks, quote equally low prices and be equally prompt and accurate in the delivery of orders, still there are few others which combine all these good points, and fewer still which possess another—that of handling only strictly reliable goods. This enterprise was inaugurated by Messrs. George H. and W. S. Brewster in 1879, under the style of Brewster Brothers, which is still retained, although the recent death of Mr. George H. Brewster left his brother sole proprietor. He is a native of this city, and is thoroughly acquainted with his business, to which he gives close personal attention. The store has an area of 1000 square feet and is heavily stocked with choice staple and fancy groceries, provisions, teas, coffees, spices, etc. Sufficient assistance is employed to ensure prompt and courteous attention to every caller and orders will be filled at the shortest possible notice, the goods being guaranteed to prove just as represented.

Chas. D. James, dealer in Fresh and Salt Meats, Beef, Pork, Lamb, Mutton, Veal, Poultry, Smoked Beef, Ham, Bacon, Sausage and Bologna, 22 Market Street, Norwich, Conn.—There are very probably but few among our readers, outside of those engaged in that line of business, who have any adequate idea of the immense amount of meat consumed in this city every week, for although it may readily be imagined that the consumption is considerable, still the real figures are much larger than one would think possible. One of the best establishments to visit in order to get a good idea of the magnitude and importance of the meat traffic, is that conducted by Mr. Charles D. James, at No. 22 Market street, for this gentleman is a very prominent dealer in fresh and salt meats, beef, pork, lamb, mutton, veal, poultry, smoked beef, ham, bacon, sausage and bologna, and does both a wholesale and retail business, principally the latter. He is a native of Griswold and has carried on his present enterprise since 1879. The premises occupied comprise three floors of the dimensions of 55×10 feet, and an immense and varied stock is carried at all times. Employment is given to four assistants, and it is worthy of note that equally polite and careful attention is given to both large and small purchasers, while the lowest market rates are quoted in every department of the business.

John M. Brewer, Pharmacist, Pure Drugs, Franklin Square, Norwich, Conn.—When deciding where to have a prescription filled it is very natural that the preference should be given to an establishment which has been successfully carried on for a score of years or so, for so prolonged a career argues the exercise of intelligent care as well as the possession of all necessary facilities. Mr. John M. Brewer has conducted his pharmacy in Franklin square since 1869, and the nature of the policy followed is indicated by the steadily increasing popularity of the enterprise. A specialty has been made from the very first of the compounding of physicians' prescriptions, and no pharmacy in town is better prepared to fill such orders promptly, accurately and cheaply. Mr. Brewer carries a heavy stock of drugs, medicines and chemicals, and his laboratory is equipped with improved and delicate apparatus, capable of positively assuring the nicest accuracy when properly used. That it is so used, the long and honorable record of the prescription department amply demonstrates, and those who wish to feel assured that the choicest ingredients and the most intelligent care are employed in the compounding of their prescriptions, can gain such assurance by patron-

izing this popular pharmacy. Fancy goods, druggists' sundries, toilet articles, etc., are well represented in the stock, and the employment of two efficient assistants assures prompt and polite attention to every caller.

Mrs. E. Austin, Domestic Bakery, 86 Franklin Street, Norwich.—Economy is a virtue beyond a doubt, but like charity, it " covers a multitude of sins," or at least a multitude of mistakes, for some people never seem to be able to practice true economy although they deny and stint themselves in a hundred ways. That it is not economical to do yourself what can be more cheaply and better done by somebody else, would seem to be plain enough for the merest child to understand, and yet there are many housekeepers who bake their own bread, cake and pastry, when they are so circumstanced that it would be much cheaper to buy these articles at a public bakery. The objection may be raised that home cookery is superior to that practiced at such an establishment, but that does not apply to the bakery conducted by Mrs. E. Austin at No. 86 Franklin street, for the cookery here will compare favorably with the best of that done in private families, and should any of our readers doubt this fact let them remember that " the proof of the pudding is the eating," and make practical trial of Mrs. Austin's productions. A full assortment of bread, cake, pastry, etc., is always on hand to choose from, and is constantly fresh and appetizing. Brown bread and baked beans Saturday night. Mrs. Austin quotes the lowest market rates, and employs three assistants.

M. A. Barber, Machinist, 22 Ferry Street, Norwich.—At first sight it may appear strange that it is more difficult to get a steam engine properly repaired than it is to buy an entirely new one, and of course in the case of slight breakdowns this is not true, but every machinist of experience will agree that, generally speaking, it requires a higher degree of skill to repair a machine than to build it. The builder of a machine has only familiar and simple operations to go through with, while the repairer is constantly having to solve new problems and to devise new combinations to attain the desired result. The high standing held by the machine shop carried on by Mr. M. A. Barber, at No. 22 Ferry street, is due in a great measure to the success met with in the repairing of steam engines of all kinds and machinery, for particular attention is given to this class of work. Mr. Barber manufactures machines of various kinds, a specialty being made of cork machinery and laundry machinery, which finds a ready sale all over the country. This business was founded more than thirty years ago by Mr. J. E. Barber, who was succeeded by the present proprietor in 1877. The shop occupies two floors of the dimensions of 50 × 35 feet, and is equipped throughout with improved machinery.

J. A. Stoddard & Son, dealers in Fine Groceries and Provisions, Fruit, Confectionery, Cigars and Tobacco, 100 Franklin Street, Norwich.—An establishment which is a marked and general favorite among families residing in its vicinity, is that carried on by Messrs. J. A. Stoddard & Son, and located at No. 100 Franklin street. This was opened in 1884, and has steadily increased in popularity until it has attained a leading position among other stores of a similar character in this section. The premises made use of are of the dimensions of 55×20 feet, and contain a varied stock which bears evidence of careful selection in every department. It comprises choice fancy and staple groceries, teas, coffees, spices, canned goods, etc., as well as a full line of provisions, fruit and vegetables, and a very desirable assortment of cigars and tobacco. This enterprising firm quotes the lowest market rates and make it an invariable rule to give every customer full value for money received. The partners are Messrs. J. A. and J. B. Stoddard, both of whom are natives of this State. They spare no pains to keep the service up to the highest standard of efficiency, and employ two assistants.

The Merchants National Bank, 71 Main Street, Norwich, Conn.—The Merchants National Bank is one of those institutions which furnish the strongest possible argument in favor of the retention of our present banking system, for although this is not perfect by any means still it is unquestionably far superior to any system that preceded it, and no system has as yet been proposed which in its practical workings would enable the record made by the Merchants National Bank to be bettered. Not that the management of that institution have made no mistakes whatever, to assert that would be equivalent to asserting that they were more than human, but the point of the matter is that no system can insure infallibility, while given intelligence, experience and public spirit, the present system is capable of yielding most beneficent results. The Merchants Bank was incorporated some fifty-five years ago, being opened as a State bank in 1834. It was re-organized under the national banking laws in 1865, and is the oldest national bank in Norwich. It has been of incalculable benefit to the various enterprises carried on in this vicinity. The policy of the management has been and is to aid local undertakings worthy of help, whenever possible, and other things being equal, to give the preference to Norwich business houses. As may readily be imagined, such a policy is bound to be popular if ably carried out, and the present popularity of the Merchants Bank proves marked ability as well as good intentions on the part of those having it in charge. We give below a list of the officers and directors, and those familiar with the business houses of this section will recognize the following names as those of men prominently identified with such concerns:

President, J. Hunt Smith.
Cashier, Charles H. Phelps.
Directors, Costello Lippitt, Chas. F. Setchel, Calvin L. Harwood, J. Hunt Smith, Geo. F. Bard, John D. Brewster, Lucius Brown, Chas. H. Phelps, E. G. Bidwell.

The bank has a capital of $100,000, and is in the very best condition financially, as may be judged from the fact that the surplus amounts to no less than $37,000.

R. Peckham, Groceries, Every Variety at Lowest Prices, 118 Water Street, Norwich, Conn.—Comparatively few of us are able to judge of the merits of groceries before using them, and even those who are competent to do so do not care to minutely examine every article submitted to them before accepting it, and therefore it is obvious that, other things being equal, the dealer who is entirely trustworthy and who takes pains to see that his customers get just what they pay for, will build up the largest as well as the most desirable patronage. This being the case there is no occasion for surprise at the great magnitude of the business done by Mr. R. Peckham, for the enterprise conducted by this gentleman was founded in 1859, by Messrs. Smith & Cottwell, came into the possession of the present proprietor in 1869, and from the very first has been managed in an able and straightforward manner. Mr. Peckham is a native of Middletown, R. I., and in view of his long experience it is superfluous to say he is thoroughly familiar with his business in every detail. He is naturally proud of the honorable record of his establishment and it will be no fault of his if the service rendered in the future is not even more economical and efficient than that extended in the past. The premises made use of are located at No. 118 Water street, and comprise two floors and a basement, of the dimensions of 55 × 25 feet. A very heavy stock of staple and fancy groceries is constantly carried, and every variety of such goods is offered at the lowest prices quoted in the market. Some wholesale trade is enjoyed but the vast bulk of the business is retail, and particular attention is paid to the requirements of families, orders being promptly delivered and every article being guaranteed to prove just as represented.

Bouquet Millinery and Fancy Goods Store, 92 Franklin Street, Norwich, Conn.—It requires a very fine window display to attract more than passing attention in these days when window dressing has been reduced to a science, and is carried on by trained professionals without regard to expense, but there is something in the exhibit commonly made in the Bouquet Millinery and Fancy Goods Store, 92 Franklin street, which attracts admiring comment from passers by, and which indicates to some degree the exquisite taste noticeable in the arrangement and execution of the millinery work coming from this popular establishment. It was opened in 1889, and the proprietors have reason to congratulate themselves on the character no less than on the extent of the patronage, for among their customers are numbered ladies who have a more than local reputation for careful and artistic dressing, and to cater successfully to such patrons is no slight proof of ability. A heavy and varied stock of millinery and fancy goods is carried at all times, the very latest foreign and domestic fashionable novelties being represented. Particular attention is paid to custom work, and the fact that from eight to nine skilled assistants have to be employed in the busy season, shows how liberally this department is patronized. Orders can generally be filled at short notice, and the prices quoted are very low considering the quality of the work turned out.

Maxson P. Lewis, wholesale and retail dealer in Sash, Doors, Blinds, Mouldings, Paints, Oils, Glass, etc., Central Wharf, Norwich.—One of the representative enterprises of this city is that conducted by Mr. Maxson P. Lewis, on Central Wharf, and this is especially worthy of prominent mention, not only by reason of its present magnitude but also because it is of very early origin, having been inaugurated over half a century ago by Mr. Joshua Shepherd. This gentleman was succeeded by Mr. F. Rogers, and he by Messrs. Fanning & Willoughby, who gave place to Willoughby & Co., and they to Messrs. Lewis & Baldwin, this firm being succeeded by Messrs. Crowell, Lewis & Co., and the present proprietor assuming sole control in 1886. He is a native of Plainfield, and is very widely known in business circles as an enterprising merchant who adheres strictly to legitimate methods. Mr. Lewis is a wholesale and retail dealer in sash, doors, blinds, mouldings, paints, oils, glass, etc., and carries a very heavy and complete stock at all times. Estimates will be cheerfully furnished on application, and as Mr. Lewis is in a position to get dependable supplies at bottom prices, and figures very closely on all plans submitted, those wishing anything in his line would do well to give him an early call. He deals largely in pure white lead, and colors dry and ground in oil, and offers a complete assortment of the very best mixed paints in the market.

S. J. Stevenson, Birds of all kinds, Confectionery, Lunch, Cigars, etc., 372 Main Street, Norwich.—The establishment of which Mr. S. J. Stevenson is the proprietor, located at No. 372 Main street, does not make any great pretensions, but still were all the business enterprises in the city to be arranged in the order of their usefulness, that carried on by Mr. Stevenson would be by no means the last on the list. As it was opened but a few months ago it has not had a chance as yet to develop to its full capacity, but it has been well received by the public, and under its present management is sure to continue to grow in popularity. The proprietor is a native of Norwich, and works hard to give prompt and efficient service to the public, giving close personal attention to every detail of his business and making it a point to treat all alike. He deals in bakers' goods, confectionery, fruits, cigars, etc., and also makes a specialty of birds of all kinds, both canaries and wild birds, also cages, bird foods, etc. Mr. Stevenson handles superior bread and pastry and renews his stock so frequently that it is always fresh and attractive. His prices are uniformly low and those who place a trial order with him are sure to call again.

NORTON & SMITH. FINE SHOES.

The cut represents an imaginary Show Window of a Shoe Store, fitted up with the fixtures of the Norwich Nickel and Brass Works.

The Norwich Nickel and Brass Works. Salesrooms, 702 Broadway, N. Y., Office and Factory at Norwich, Conn. Catalogues on application.—Even the least observant of our readers can hardly have failed to notice the great improvement which has taken place in the character of show window displays within the past few years, for the changes which have been brought about are equivalent to a revolution, the whole art of window dressing having undergone a vigorous revival. What is known as "transient trade" is very largely influenced by the window display mode, and even regular customers are apt to desert an establishment which allows itself to be outstripped by its competitors in this respect. Good taste is of course essential to the proper arrangement of a show window, but many who fail to produce a satisfactory effect, do so not because they don't know how to arrange their goods, but rather because they lack the necessary facilities to display them attractively without injury. Therefore the appliances manufactured by the Norwich Nickel and Brass Works are worthy of the careful inspection of every store-keeper, for these include frames and stands in nickel and brass of convenient and ornamental design; the styles being exclusively confined to this concern. These frames are especially adapted to the use of dealers in men's furnishings, fancy dry goods, hats, caps and furs, boots and shoes, etc., and are sold at prices that put them within the means of every business man. Their new and elegant illustrated catalogue and manual of window dressing combined in one book, will be cheerfully sent on application to any responsible merchant, and all orders will be given prompt and careful attention. The office and factory are located in this city, the salesrooms being at No. 702 Broadway, N. Y. This business was founded about 1874, and was carried on under the style of the Norwich Nickel Works until January 1, 1889. Electro-plating on all metals is done in first class style and at very short notice. The premises utilized comprise three floors of the dimensions of about 100×36 feet each. The proprietor is Mr. William A. Aiken, who gives careful personal supervision to affairs and proposes to fully maintain the leading position now held by his products throughout the country.

Bruce & Baird, Boots, Shoes and Rubbers, 114 Main Street, Norwich, Conn.—Among the many enterprising concerns engaged in the retailing of boots, shoes and rubbers in Norwich and vicinity we know of none which is more active, more reliable or more generally popular than that of Bruce & Baird, doing business at No. 114 Main street, and the universal popularity of this firm is all the more significant from the fact that they have carried on operations here for a score of years—certainly long enough for the residents of this section to become thoroughly familiar with their facilities and their methods. The business was founded many years before the present proprietors assumed control, in 1870, and indeed is one of the oldest established enterprises of the kind in this vicinity. Mr. Bruce was born in Brimfield, Mass., removed to Webster in 1849, he at one time held the position of town clerk, and in Norwich has been secretary West Chelsea board of education for five years. He is a member of the Odd Fellows, the Knights of Pythias, and the American Mechanics; while Mr. Baird, his partner, is a native of Milford, Ct., and is connected with the Free Masons and the Grand Army. Both members of the firm give close personal attention to customers, and callers will find that the phrase "light expenses, low prices," as used by this concern means something, for no lower prices are quoted in this portion of the State on dependable foot-wear than Messrs. Bruce & Baird are prepared to name. Their stock is "clean" in every department, and comprises full lines of staple goods in addition to the very latest novelties in fashionable foot-wear. Callers are assured prompt and polite attention, and buyers have the satisfaction of knowing that every article is fully guaranteed to prove as represented.

John P. Barstow & Co., dealers in Stoves, Furnaces, Ranges; Seeds, Farm Implements and Fertilizers, Nos. 23 and 25 Water Street, Norwich, Conn.—Mr. John P. Barstow is thoroughly identified with the sale of stoves, ranges, furnaces, etc., if anyone in this city is, for he has dealt in such articles for not far from half a century, beginning operations in 1846 as a member of the firm of I. Backus & Co. The style afterwards became Backus & Barstow, then Barstow & Palmer, Mr. Barstow then assumed sole control, the present partnership being formed in 1876, by the association of Messrs. John P. Barstow, Frank H. Smith and George S. Byles. The firm do an immense business, both wholesale and retail, and carry a tremendous stock, as is evidenced by the size of the premises utilized, these comprising one building having four floors of the dimensions of 35 × 60 feet, and two buildings containing three floors measuring 40 × 70 feet. Stoves, furnaces and ranges of the most improved type may be bought at the lowest market rates at this time-honored establishment, for it goes without saying that Messrs. John P. Barstow & Co. are prepared to offer exceptional inducements to customers, as they enjoy the most favorable relations with manufacturers and do business on a very liberal basis. Farm implements are also very extensively dealt in, together with fertilizers and seeds of standard merit, these commodities being supplied in quantities to suit, without delay, and being guaranteed to give the best of satisfaction when properly used. Employment is given to five competent assistants, and the members of the firm give careful personal attention to the supervision of affairs, sparing no pains to fully maintain the enviable reputation of this representative establishment.

F. W. Tracy, dealer in Meats, Groceries, 30 Main Street, Preston, Conn.—In analyzing the popularity that the enterprise carried on by Mr. F. W. Tracy unquestionably enjoys, we find that it does not seem to be due to any one thing, but rather, to the impression made by his methods of doing business, when considered altogether. For instance, Mr. Tracy does not claim to sell cheaper than everybody else, although he does offer his goods at the lowest market rates. Neither does he claim to carry the largest stock in this section of the town, but nevertheless the variety on hand is such that all tastes can be suited. He strives to fully satisfy every customer and give a dollar's worth of value for every dollar he receives, and it may be said that this is probably one of the chief causes of the popularity referred to. Mr. F. W. Tracy is a native of Preston and has had considerable experience in his present business. He has been sole proprietor of the establishment since 1883, at that time succeeding Mr. John Tracy who had carried it on for over forty years. The premises utilized are located at No. 30 Main street, and are 50 × 25 feet in dimensions, and contain an extensive and varied stock of meats and groceries in general. All classes of trade are catered to, the prices are placed at the lowest figures consistent with the handling of dependable goods, and prompt and courteous attention is assured to every caller, there being two competent and polite assistants employed.

B. H. Palmer, dealer in Dry Goods, Fine Groceries, Boots and Shoes, Crockery, etc. Satisfaction guaranteed. 398 and 400 North Main Street, Norwich, Conn.—The establishment now conducted by Mr. B. H. Palmer, was opened in 1863, by the firm of Main & Palmer, and in 1864 the present proprietor, Mr. B. H. Palmer, assumed full and entire management of the business, and it is safe to say was never more generally popular than has been the case during the past year. He is a native of Lisbon, Conn., and is universally known throughout Norwich and vicinity. His establishment would not be one half so well patronized as it now is unless the inducements extended were of a solid and genuine character. The stock on hand embraces a skillfully chosen assortment of merchandise, and so varied and complete is it that there are few articles in common family use that is not included within it. Mr. Palmer is a shrewd and successful buyer and pursues the policy of sharing the advantages so gained with his patrons. The public have long since learned that a dollar will go at least as far at this store as at any similar establishment in this vicinity and they have also learned that all representations made can be implicitly relied upon. This establishment is located at Nos. 398 and 400 North Main street, and contains an extensive stock of dry goods, fine groceries, boots and shoes, crockery, etc. Three reliable assistants are constantly employed, and the details of the business which is both wholesale and retail is most ably handled. "Honesty is the best policy," according to the proverb, and certainly the success attained by the enterprise under mention would seem to prove that "sharp practice" is by no means essential to the building up of a large and permanent trade.

Charles E. Gaskell, Pharmacist, North Main, corner Fifth Street, Norwich, Conn.—People are very apt to wonder how the proprietor of a "general store" can keep track of all the articles he handles, and are not slow to excuse the frequent mistakes made in such establishments, on the grounds that errors are unavoidable under such circumstances, and yet we question if the average general store contains a much larger variety of articles than may be found in a first-class modern pharmacy. Such a one for instance as is conducted by Charles E. Gaskell, at the corner of North Main and Fifth streets. The extreme rarity of errors in a well equipped drug store speaks volumes for the ability and care of those having such establishments in charge, but the public accept this condition of affairs as a matter of course and give but little credit to those to whom credit is due. Mr. Gaskell carries a very large and varied stock, including an extremely complete assortment of drugs, medicines and chemicals of every description. Special attention is given to prescription trade and no pains is spared to fill all orders in this department in an absolutely accurate manner, and at very reasonable prices. The store is 25 × 35 feet in dimensions, and contains in addition to the goods already mentioned, a fine stock of toilet and fancy articles, druggists' sundries, etc. Mr. Gaskell is a native of Munson, Mass. He established his present undertaking in 1885, under the firm name of Gaskell & Fitzpatrick, and six months after assumed the entire control and management of the business, which he has largely developed since that date.

Utley's Printing Office, Artistic Printing of all kinds, 111 Water Street, Norwich.—Practically everybody is interested in knowing where orders for printing may be placed in the full assurance that they will be filled in the most artistic manner at short notice, for the business public need bill-heads, letter-heads, etc., those active in social circles often require ball programs, etc., and wedding invitations and other jobs of fine printing are in constant and general demand. The familiar maxim "the best is the cheapest" has a very wide application, but is especially worthy of being borne in mind when one is placing orders for printing, as the public have become so accustomed to first-class typographical work of late as to be quick to observe any lowering of the standard. Good taste of course demands that the ball programs, wedding invitations, etc., should not give the least evidence of "cheapness" in their appearance, and sound business policy as strongly demands the avoidance of the same appearance in bill-heads and other commercial printing, for a "cheap" bill or letter head argues a "cheap" firm and *vice versa.* At Utley's Printing Office a specialty of artistic printing is made, and this establishment at No. 111 Water street, can therefore be unreservedly recommended to our readers who will find it thoroughly well equipped in every respect, and the management all that could be desired. Careful personal attention is given to every order and five assistants are employed, the facilities at hand being such as to admit of commissions being executed at exceptionally short notice in cases where haste is essential.

John P. Murphy, dealer in Fine Groceries and Provisions, 4 West Main Street, Norwich, Conn.—Main street is a very busy thoroughfare and there are many well-equipped grocery houses located upon it, but among these there is not one more deserving of the popularity it has attained than is that conducted by Mr. John P. Murphy. The business in question was founded a good many years ago, having been carried on for a long time by Mr. P. D. Murphy, who was succeeded by the present proprietor in 1878. The premises made use of are located at No. 4 West Main street, and are very spacious, two floors of the dimensions of 50×40 feet being occupied, giving a total area of 4000 square feet. The stock is in harmony with the premises, for it is very extensive and is so complete in every department that no trouble is met with in suiting all tastes and all purses. Mr. Murphy caters especially to family trade, and obtains his supplies from the most reputable sources thus being in a position to guarantee satisfaction to his customers both as regards the quality and the price of the goods offered. These include not only groceries and provisions of all kinds, but also as fine an assortment of pure liquors, wines, etc., as the city can show. No fancy prices are quoted, but the articles are guaranteed to prove as represented, and prompt and courteous attention is assured to every caller.

Norwich Steam Laundry Company, all kinds of work received; Faultless Work, Perfect Satisfaction or no Pay Required; Collars and Cuffs two cents each; S. & J. Gregson, Proprietors, 193 Franklin Street, Norwich, Conn.— The enterprise conducted by the Norwich Steam Laundry Company is rapidly and steadily gaining in popularity and patronage under its present management, and for reasons so obvious that they must be apparent even to the most careless observer. The objections commonly raised against the ordinary public laundry, are that the work is sometimes only partially done, the goods are apt to be injured by chemicals or by improper handling, and the delivery is uncertain. None of these apply to the establishment in question, the proprietors of which guarantee perfect satisfaction or no pay and are prepared to carry out that guarantee to the letter. All kinds of work are received, for the laundry is equipped with the most improved machinery, skilled and careful assistants are employed and in short the facilities at hand are fully equal to the best. This enterprise was inaugurated in January, 1887, by Messrs. S. & J.

Gregson, and was originally located at No. 51 Shetucket street, but has since been removed to the present more commodious quarters at No. 193 Franklin street. These comprise two floors of the dimensions of 80 × 40 feet, and are so admirably arranged as to obviate all confusion, and make any errors in the handling and delivery of work of very rare occurrence. Both partners give close personal attention to the business and spare no pains to maintain the service at the very highest standard. Very reasonable rates are quoted, and those who place a trial order at this establishment are sure to become regular patrons.

Powers Brothers, dealers in Fresh Fish, Oysters, Clams, Lobsters and Vegetables, New Place, No. 10 Rose Place, Norwich, Conn.—It is considered as one of the axioms of business that excellent goods can always be obtained by those who are willing to pay for them, but as a matter of fact this does not invariably prove to be the case, for there is doubtless not one among our readers but what has found difficulty at times in securing first-class goods at any price. Take it in the matter of fish alone and every experienced purchaser knows that there are dealers who, while quoting the highest market rates, still do not handle really first-class goods excepting occasionally. On the other hand there are some who follow an opposite policy, and among these must justly be placed the firm of Powers Brothers, for this concern spare no pains to supply their customers with the choicest goods obtainable, and at the same time quote prices which will compare very favorably with those of dealers by no means so careful in this respect. Messrs. Powers Brothers began operations in 1881, and have built up a thriving and desirable trade. The partners are Messrs. R. M., and J. T. Powers, the former being a native of Norwich and the latter of Michigan. Two floors of the dimensions of 45 × 20 feet are occupied, at No. 10 Rose Place, and the stock on hand comprises all kinds of fresh fish in their season, together with oysters, clams, lobsters and vegetables. It is safe to say that when this firm cannot supply a certain article in the line of fish it is not to be had in the Norwich market, and it is also safe to assert that at no establishment in the city is better value given for money received.

Breed Hall Ladies' and Gents' Restaurant, Randall & Hewitt, Proprietors. Regular Dinner, 35 cents. 14 Main Street, Norwich, Conn.— It is often said that "The way to a man's heart is through his stomach," and certain it is that we are so constituted that an appetizing and abundant meal has a wonderful effect in making us feel at peace with all mankind, while on the contrary a badly prepared or scanty dinner is very apt to stir up whatever ugliness there may be lying dormant in our breasts. Therefore we feel that we are doing something towards making mankind happier when we call attention to the service rendered at the Breed Hall Ladies' and Gents' Restaurant, for the proprietors of this establishment not only believe in feeding their guests well but have the facilities and ability to do so to the best advantage. The premises are 75 × 55 feet in dimensions, and are very completely fitted up, being supplied with every facility to enhance the comfort and convenience of patrons. Messrs. Randall & Hewitt, the proprietors of this popular restaurant, have carried it on since 1885 and deserve unstinted commendation for their intelligent efforts to cater to all their tastes, and their policy of producing substantial and palatable food at prices satisfactory to the most economically disposed. Both members of the firm are natives of Preston, and both give the many details of their business careful personal attention, the result being that the service is maintained at the highest standard of efficiency and the popularity of the enterprise is constantly and rapidly increasing. The bill of fare is so varied that all tastes can be suited, and the regular dinner provided for 35 cents is a marvel of cheapness considering the variety and excellence of the viands it comprises.

Miss A. S. Mitchell, Millinery and Fancy Goods, 10 Shetucket Street, Norwich.—It is difficult and in fact practically impossible to give an idea of the nature of the inducements offered at the establishment conducted by Miss A. S. Mitchell, at No. 10 Shetucket street, within the limited space at our command, for the lady in question deals in millinery and fancy goods and any verbal description of such articles must, even under the most favorable circumstances, be inadequate and unsatisfactory. She utilizes very spacious premises, the store being 85×30 feet in dimensions and carries an unusually extensive and varied stock comprising the very latest fashionable novelties in the way of millinery goods, ribbons, velvets, laces, flowers and other trimmings, besides a very carefully selected assortment of fancy goods. Miss Mitchell will supply both trimmed and untrimmed hats and bonnets, but makes a leading specialty of custom work and even during the height of the season can fill orders at comparatively short notice, for at such times she employs fifteen experienced assistants and of course can handle a great deal of business. No more tasteful or thorough millinery work is done in this city, and as Miss Mitchell's prices are moderate it is not at all surprising that her business should be steadily increasing.

N. Tarrant, Real Estate and Insurance Agent, No. 45 Main Street, Norwich —The real estate branch of the business conducted by Mr. N. Tarrant was founded in 1870 and the insurance department was added in 1886, so that the public have had ample opportunity to become conversant with Mr. Tarrant's methods and to judge intelligently concerning his facilities and ability. That the verdict is distinctly favorable is evidenced by the present magnitude of his business, and indeed but few inquiries are necessary in order to demonstrate the fact that Mr. Tarrant is considered a competent authority on real estate matters, making his co-operation of great value to those seeking dependable and "inside" information concerning this class of property. His office is located at No. 45 Main street, and as he always has on his books some very desirable real estate to sell, rent or exchange, those wishing to invest in, to dispose of, or to hire a house, store or tenement, may save themselves time, trouble and perhaps money by taking advantage of the facilities here provided. Information will be cheerfully and courteously given and we are confident our readers will have reason to thank us for calling their attention to this well-equipped and popular agency. Mr. Tarrant represents the American Insurance Co. of Newark, N. J., the Norwich Union, of Norwich, England, and the Scottish Union of Edinburgh, Scotland, and is prepared to write policies at the very lowest market rates on "insurance that insures."

H. D. Avery, dealer in Choice Groceries, Fruit and Pastry, 202 Franklin Street, Norwich, Conn.—There is no difficulty in deciding what position to assign the establishment conducted by Mr. H. D. Avery when classing it among the many retail grocery stores to be found in this city, for even on the most superficial examination it becomes evident that this must be given a prominent and leading place, and the only result of more careful investigation is to strengthen its claim to such a position. Mr. Avery was born in Poquonnoc, Conn., and has been identified with his present business for about a decade. He occupies spacious and well arranged premises at No. 202 Franklin street, and carries as attractive an assortment of family stores as this city can show. It is made up of choice staple and fancy groceries, foreign and domestic fruit, and superior pastry, and is so complete in its several departments that it is obvious all tastes are catered to. Mr. Avery employs two efficient and courteous assistants, and spares no pains to assure prompt and polite attention to every caller. He delivers goods free to any part of the city, and this service is so reliable that when an article is promised at a certain time it will surely be forthcoming—a fact appreciated by all experienced housekeepers. The prices are in strict accordance with the lowest market rates, so that economy as well as convenience is served by

J. A. Hiscox, Architect, 12 Shetucket Street.—That the services of a competent architect are, as a general thing, worth several times what they cost, is a fact upon which practically all who have had experience in building are agreed, and therefore we will not stop to set forth the advantages to be derived from the employment of such aid, but will proceed at once to call attention to the facilities possessed by Mr. James A. Hiscox, whose office is located at No. 12 Shetucket street, for this gentleman is prepared to undertake any thing in the line of architectural designing, etc., and his record is such as to assure entire satisfaction to customers. He was associated from 1887 to October, 1889, with Mr. E. A. Cudworth, and enjoys an enviable reputation for giving close and skillful attention to the interests of clients. Those wishing information concerning building, alterations, specifications, drawings or decorative designs of all kinds, may profitably consult Mr. Hiscox, who is prepared to furnish complete supervision including all necessary working drawings, details, scale drawing, tracings, blue prints, estimates, specifications and contracts at a very reasonable percentage. Should any of our readers contemplate building or alterations they would do well to call on Mr. Hiscox, who will make them sketches and estimates, and a perspective in color or ink, giving a correct idea of how the work will look when completed. There are many details to be settled upon before building operations can be begun, and much time, trouble and expense may be saved by consulting an architect at the earliest possible moment so as to have an opportunity to study the plans before making definite choice. The following residences were erected under the personal supervision of Mr. Hiscox: The residence of Mr. F. H. Smith on Washington street (see illustration elsewhere), and Mrs. Loomis' at East Great Plains. Among those erected since, we would mention the following : Dr. Clapp's on East Broad street, Mrs. Roath's on Hamlin, and Dr. Brewer's six new houses on Oak street. He has also erected a number of fine buildings in neighboring towns, among which are Mr. Whiting's residence in New London, Stonington school building (costing $30,000), and a number of sea shore cottages at Eastern Point and Watch Hill. Mr. Hiscox also gives prompt attention to communications by mail, and will at once wait upon those who find it inconvenient to call at his office.

J. G. Standish, dealer in Harness, Trunks, Bags, Rubber and Oiled Clothing, 115 Main Street, Norwich, Conn. —Mr. John G. Standish conducts an enterprise which demands prominent mention in these columns, both on account of the length of time it has been in operation and the leading position it now holds among similar undertakings in this section. It was inaugurated just about half a century ago, by Messrs. Warren & Standish and was continued by Messrs. Standish & Barnes, finally coming into the sole possession of the present owner in 1850. He was born in Hebron, Conn., and has long been ranked high among the business men of this city. The premises made use of are located at No. 115 Main street, and have an area of about 1200 square feet, affording ample room for the accommodation of a large assortment of harness, trunks, bags, rubber and oiled clothing, etc., as well as for a well-appointed shop in which custom work and repairing are done in a superior manner at short notice. Considering his long experience it is hardly necessary to say that Mr. Standish is in a position to sell dependable goods as cheap as anybody can, and considering the enviable reputation of his enterprise it seems almost superfluous to add that every article bought at this establishment is sure to prove precisely as represented in every respect.

The Ossawan Mills Company, manufacturers of Braided and Twisted Worsted, Silk, Cotton and Wire Cords, and of the Crown Solid Braided Cord, 185 East Broad Street, Norwich, Conn.—Few of those not immediately connected with the business in one form or another have any idea of the enormous consumption of picture, shade and furniture cords, but it is a subject in which the residents of Norwich should take particular interest from the fact that one of the oldest established and most truly representative of our city factories is devoted to this branch of production, and ranks as the most prominent establishment of the kind in the country. We refer to the business carried on by the Ossawan Mills Company, this having been founded in 1859 by Mr. John Turner, who conducted it for a score of years, being succeeded by the present company in 1879. The factory building erected in 1861 has been several times materially enlarged and it is significant of the continued prosperity of the company that further addition is to be made in the immediate future, a commodious structure now being in process of erection. It has ever been the policy of the management to keep fully up to the times as regards their mechanical equipment, and as a natural consequence the plant of machinery now in use is composed of the latest improved appliances and is unsurpassed for accuracy and general efficiency of operation. Both steam and water are utilized as motive powers and the annual product is very large in amount and great in value, it comprising braided and twisted silk, cotton, worsted and wire cords, for pictures, shades, furniture, etc., a great variety of sizes and styles being made, and the goods being accepted as the standard in their special lines wherever introduced. Specialties are made of braided and twisted wire and the Crown solid braided cord, this latter having a national reputation for uniform strength and durability. The company employ fifty assistants, and when the contemplated addition to their factory is completed (which will probably be before this article is put into print) they will be prepared to fill orders more promptly than ever and to offer a greatly improved service in many ways. The goods are shipped to every portion of the world and are highly esteemed both by dealers and consumers, as they prove as represented and consequently give uniform satisfaction. The company are in a position to quote bottom prices as well as to furnish goods of unsurpassed quality. This enterprise is properly in the hands of representative Connecticut business men; the treasurer being Mr. Elisha Turner; the president, Mr. F. C. Turner; and the secretary Mr. E. P. Turner. They give close personal attention to the supervision of affairs and are evidently determined to fully maintain the enviable reputation their undertaking has held so long.

John Troland, dealer in Plumbing Goods and Gas Fixtures, Stoves, Ranges and Furnaces, Plumbing, Gas Fitting, Tin Roofing and Jobbing of all kinds, 23 West Main street, Norwich, Conn. — The business now carried on by Mr. John Troland was founded some thirty years ago, it having been inaugurated by Mr. James Troland in 1859. Troland Brothers assumed control in 1873, and were succeeded by the present proprietor in 1878. He is a native of Norwich, and is one of the best known men in his line

of business in the city. The premises made use of are located at No. 23 West Main street, and contain a very extensive and carefully chosen stock of plumbing goods and gas fixtures, stoves, ranges and furnaces, for Mr. Troland deals largely in these and similar articles and is prepared to fill both wholesale and retail orders at short notice and at the very lowest market rates. He handles cooking and heating apparatus of the most improved type and is in a position to guarantee satisfaction to those who will acquaint him with their wants and allow him to select the kind best suited to their needs. Employment is given to four assistants, and plumbing, gas fitting, tin roofing and general jobbing will be done in a thorough and workmanlike manner at short notice. We would call special attention to Mr. Troland's facilities to do plumbing, for such work must be skillfully and honestly carried out or the consequences may be serious, and the most absolute confidence may safely be placed in that done under Mr. Troland's direction.

___

Mrs. S. M. Howie, dealer in Fancy Goods, Toys, Jewelry, Glassware and Housekeeping Goods. Picture Framing a Specialty. 96 Main Street, Norwich, Conn.—The establishment conducted by Mrs. S. M. Howie at No. 96 Main street, has long been a prime favorite with the purchasing public, and its popularity is so thoroughly well deserved that we take pleasure in making favorable mention of this excellently managed enterprise The business was founded about a decade ago by Mr. J. E. Stewart, and passed under the control of Mrs. Howie in 1886. The store is very conveniently fitted up and contains as carefully chosen a stock as can be found in this city, for Mrs. Howie is an experienced and discriminating buyer and is very successful in selecting just such articles as her customers require. The assortment is so varied and so abundant that detailed mention of it is impossible in these columns, but some idea of its character and completeness may be gained from the fact that it comprises fancy goods, toys, jewelry, glassware and housekeeping goods. The latest novelties are well represented and the prices are in every instance in strict accordance with the lowest market rates. A specialty is made of picture framing, such work being done to order in a superior manner at short notice. All styles of plain and fancy frames are made and the results attained cannot fail to satisfy the most critical. Callers are assured immediate and courteous attention at all times, goods being invariably warranted to prove just as represented.

___

Hamilton & Pratt, Fine Mercantile Printers. Fine Work and Prompt Attention. 103 Broadway, Norwich, Conn.— There are a few business men who claim that such "trifling details," as they call them, as the printing of bill and letter heads, cards, etc., are unworthy of serious attention, as the public don't care a snap what kind of cards or bill heads a firm uses as long as they sell dependable goods at bottom prices, but this is a very short-sighted view of the matter, and one which if logically carried out would put a stop to the building of elegant stores, the artistic dressing of show windows and the many other deferences paid to the universal habit of judging largely from appearances. The standing of a firm is judged by the character of the printing sent out, much as the standing of an individual is estimated from his dress or from the appearance of his visiting-cards, and although a worthy and well-bred person may in rare instances be satisfied to use too showy or too mean looking apparel or stationery, still the chances are all the other way. There are styles in printing as in everything else, and in order to be sure of being fully "up with the times," it is an excellent idea to place your orders with such a firm as that of Hamilton & Pratt, for they make it a rule to keep their office well supplied with the latest novelties in type, etc., and are looked upon as authorities in all that concerns mercantile and job printing in general. The premises utilized are located at No. 103 Broadway and are equipped with the most improved and efficient presses, etc., while employment is given to a sufficiently large force to enable the most extensive orders to be filled at very short notice when haste is particularly required. Messrs. Hamilton & Pratt are uniformly moderate in their prices, and we can unreservedly guarantee that all work will give entire satisfaction.

H. M. Durfey, Fine Groceries, Provisions, Flour, Grain, Feed, Fruits, Vegetables, Crockery, Glass, and Wooden-Ware, Corner of Central Avenue and Seventh Street, (Greeneville), Norwich, Conn.—There is no need of our saying that the undertaking now conducted by Mr. H. M. Durfey is one of Greeneville's representative enterprises for the fact is too well known to require argument or even statement. Mr. Durfey was born in Greeneville, where he is the oldest native-born resident, and began operations here in 1882, having at that time succeeded Mr. T. D. Phillips. During the eight years that the establishment has been under Mr. Durfey's management it has maintained its position among the leading enterprises of a similar character. The premises utilized are located at the corner of Central avenue and Seventh street and comprise a store 50×50 feet in dimensions. Fine groceries, provisions, flour, grain, feed, fruits, vegetables, etc., are handled very largely, and crockery, glass and wooden-ware are also extensively dealt in As might naturally be supposed in the case of so old established an enterprise, the most favorable relations are enjoyed with producers and wholesalers, buying everything for cash, and as a consequence the inducements offered to customers are many and pronounced. Three competent assistants are employed and all orders are filled with the utmost promptness, the quality of the goods being in all cases guaranteed to prove as represented. Mr. Durfey is thoroughly conversant with every detail of his business, and gives close personal attention to its supervision, rendering truly valuable service to the public by conducting a first-class establishment and offering reliable goods at fair prices. Mr. Durfey has served three years in the army and since then has taken a great interest in G. A. R. affairs. Has been for twenty-three years a member of the relief committee of Sedgwick Post No. 1 G. A. R. Has also been for a number of years a notary public and gives his services as such to veterans and their families gratuitously. Has served two years in common council and has been an officer in the Connecticut department of G. A. R.

___

S. L. Geer, Dentist, 59 Broadway, Norwich, Conn.—If people would spend half as much money on their teeth as they do on articles calculated to injure or destroy them, a sound, white and even set of teeth would not be a rarity, but in spite of the warnings, counsels and examples given by those in a position to instruct the public on this point, the majority of the community will still persist in eating and drinking what they should not, in failing to give their teeth proper attention, and in short in abusing these useful servants steadily and badly. The consequence finally is that they rebel. Suddenly a violent toothache begins; the sufferer is astonished that such an infliction should come upon him "without cause," and probably, finally accounts for it by ascribing it to a cold—as if sound, healthy teeth could be made to ache by any cold or exposure. It pays to keep the teeth in good condition, and failing to do this, it pays to consult a competent dentist on the first symptom of trouble. Should a tooth begin to ache don't put off visiting the dentist until the pain has continued so long as to have become unbearable, until the gums have become swollen and sensitive and the entire nervous system has been put "on edge," but go at once. Either that tooth should be extracted, or it should be filled, and in either case "delays are dangerous." There is no lack of competent dentists in this city, but it is safe to say not one of them is better known or has enjoyed a larger experience than Dr. S. L. Geer, located at 59 Broadway. This gentleman has practised his profession for thirty years and has made a most favorable impression since beginning operations in Norwich. His office is fitted up with the most improved apparatus and tools, and the most difficult operations can be performed in an entirely satisfactory manner. Gentle but thorough methods are practised, and as the charges are uniformly moderate we can unhesitatingly recommend this office to all in need of the services of an experienced and skilful dental practitioner.

John C. Perkins, Manufacturing Confectioner, Perkins Block, 202 Main Street, Norwich, Conn.—Without question the representative establishment of its kind in this section is that conducted by Mr. John C. Perkins in Perkins Block, Main street, and it is no discredit to other houses in a similar line of business that such should be the case, for the enterprise to which we have reference was inaugurated many years ago and has been conducted with marked ability almost from its inception. Operations were begun in 1859 by Mr. David L. Gale, he being followed by Messrs. S. B. and H. G. Ransom, who gave place to Mr. H. G. Ransom, who was succeeded by Messrs. Perkins & Root; the present proprietor assuming sole control in 1864. He built the elegant edifice now occupied, in 1871, the premises comprising five floors of the dimensions of 75 × 33 feet. Mr. Perkins is a manufacturing confectioner, and utilizes one of the most completely equipped factories in New England. He does a very heavy wholesale and retail business and has a most enviable reputation for offering strictly reliable goods at the very lowest market rates. Among the more prominent specialties handled may be mentioned the celebrated " English Wafer Lozenges," which have gained such great and abiding popularity. Mr. Perkins was the first and the originator who introduced these elegant goods into this market and his products have never been *successfully* imitated although many attempts have been made to do so. Employment is afforded to ten competent assistants, and every caller is assured immediate and courteous attention.

The Howe Cement Co., manufacturers of Fine Shoe Dressings, 32 Talman Street, Norwich, Conn. —It will never be known exactly how many thousands of dollars have been spent in the improvement of cements for leather, rubber, etc., but the total sum must be very large indeed for almost numberless attempts have been made to discover new compounds, and experiments have been carried on for prolonged periods and almost without regard to expense. The ideal cement is unaffected by moisture or a reasonable degree of heat, hardens quickly, but not too quickly, is easily applied and contains no ingredient in the least degree harmful to leather or rubber. In the opinion of many practical men and thoroughly competent judges, the compounds produced by the Howe Cement Company more nearly approach this ideal than any others in the market, and the proof of this is to be found in the large and rapidly increasing demand for the company's goods. Operations were begun in 1874, and the business has increased until now three floors of dimensions averaging 40 × 25 feet each are utilized for manufacturing purposes, and employment is given to a number of experienced assistants. The office and factory are located at No. 32 Talman street, and are equipped with all necessary facilities for the manufacture of leather and rubber cements, thus enabling orders to be filled at short notice and at moderate rates. The company also manufacture the celebrated Daisy Shoe Polish which is warranted perfectly harmless to ladies' and children's fine shoes and gives a durable and brilliant gloss. It is put up in attractive form, and if desired it can be procured in a wooden safety box which prevents breakage. They also manufacture the Eagle Dressing, which is equally harmless and the best ten cent dressing made. The proprietors are Messrs. S. G. and W. R. Howe, the former being a native of Maine and the latter of Massachusetts.

Brewster & Burnett, Stoves, Tin Ware, Agricultural Implements, Seeds of all kinds. Sole Agents for the "Good News" and "Magee" Ranges. Tin Roofing and General Jobbing, 5 and 7 Water Street, Norwich, Conn.—The comparative standing of a business house can generally be quite accurately judged from the character of the articles for which it acts as agent, for the manufacturers of goods of national reputation are not liable to risk their good name by putting them in the hands of any but first-class concerns. Therefore when we say that Messrs. Brewster & Burnett are sole agents for the "Good News " and the "Magee " ranges we have already established their claim to a leading position among other houses in their line of business, for it goes without saying that these ranges have no superiors in the market to-day. Messrs. Brewster & Burnett began operations in 1881, and as both partners were thoroughly familiar with the practical details of their business and were determined to offer the best possible service to the public, it is no wonder that they soon attained a flattering degree of success or that the business should have continued to steadily increase. The premises made use of comprise five floors of the dimensions of 85 × 40 feet, and are located at Nos. 5 and 7 Water street. The stock includes not only stoves but also tin ware, agricultural implements, seeds of all kinds, etc., and is so extensive and so carefully selected that all orders, either wholesale or retail, can be filled without delay. Employment is given to six competent assistants, and tin roofing and general jobbing will be done in a superior manner at the lowest market rates, under the personal supervision of either E. M. Brewster or W. H. Burnett. The former is a native of Griswold, Conn., and has been connected with the board of aldermen, while Mr. Burnett was born in Scotland, Conn., and, like his partner, is extremely well known personally in this section.

Troy Steam Laundry, 145 Little Water Street, Norwich, Conn.—That public laundries have "come to stay " is of course evident to even the least observing person, but those who are not especially interested in the matter have no idea of the rapidity with which the practice of sending family washings to such establishments is spreading,—a rapidity so great that it is apparently only a question of a few years when practically every ordinarily well-to-do family will adopt this course. It certainly has much to commend it, and it receives the powerful aid of physicians of all schools, who agree that doing the family washing at home is a fruitful cause of disease, for reasons which should be obvious to every intelligent person. There are public laundries unworthy of patronage no doubt, but these are the marked exceptions, the majority of such establishments being honorably and skillfully managed. Prominent among this latter class should be placed the Troy Steam Laundry located at No. 145 Little Water street, for the work done here is equal to the best ; the finest fabrics are not injured in handling ; the service is prompt and reliable, and the charges are uniformly moderate. The manager has had long practical experience in his present line of business and is consequently well qualified to attain thoroughly satisfactory results. The premises utilized comprise two floors of the dimensions of 65 × 55 feet and are fitted up with the very latest improved machinery, driven by a six horse engine. Employment is given to six competent assistants.

Mr. Charles A. Burnham, who had carried on the business since 1880. The premises utilized are 75 × 25 feet in dimensions and contain all necessary facilities and appliances for the making of blank books, the ruling of paper to any desired pattern, and book binding of all descriptions. Particular attention is paid to the accurate numbering to order of checks, notes, coupons, drafts and tickets of all kinds in any colored ink desired, and another important feature of the business is the binding of all magazines, periodicals and newspapers in any style that may be preferred. Back numbers will be furnished to complete volumes, and the charges made are uniformly moderate. Old books will be repaired and rebound in a neat and durable fashion, and a specialty is made of fine lettering in gold or silver, on moroccos, silks, satins or velvets. Estimates are cheerfully furnished and prompt and careful attention is given to every order.

Wauregan House, Ober & Leland, Proprietors, Norwich, Conn.—Of all the varied information given in this book concerning Norwich and her interests, probably none will be more highly appreciated by out-of-town readers (among whom the bulk of its circulation will probably be had) than that relating to hotel accommodations; for those who contemplate a visit to this city for the first time or after an interval of years, will of course turn to its pages for counsel concerning which house it is best to put up at. Now, it is often difficult to properly advise even a personal friend in this matter; for "different people have different tastes" and what may suit you may prove objectionable to another and vice-versa, but still we have no hesitation in recommending the Wauregan House, for the simple reason that it is a city hotel, run on metropolitan principles and the policy of its management is consequently acceptable to all classes of patrons. You may be as quiet as you please within its walls, or you may mix in with enjoyable, congenial company, and in either event you are sure of receiving respectful treatment from the *attachés* of the house and of "getting your money's worth," as the saying is, in every respect. The Wauregan House is a handsome five-story building, having a frontage of 85 feet on Main street, and 120 feet on Broadway. It contains about 100 guest rooms, and is equipped with all necessary facilities for comfort and recreation. From thirty to forty assistants are employed, and guests are served with a promptness and politeness which might very profitably be imitated at other hotels which could be mentioned. For the further accommodation of patrons, extensive improvements are contemplated, among which is enlarging the office to twice its present size and taking an adjoining store for the barber shop which will be one of the finest in the State. The present proprietors, Messrs. Ober & Leland, have been in charge for some years and have made the Wauregan pleasantly familiar to hosts of travelers. They spare no pains to satisfy every reasonable guest, and the terms of the house are remarkably low considering the accommodations provided.

Joseph Bradford, Practical Blank Book manufacturer, Paper Ruler and Book Binder, 85 Main Street, Bulletin Building, Norwich, Conn.—It is sometimes of no small importance to know the address of one who is prepared to make blank books of all kinds to order at short notice and at moderate rates, and our readers would do well to note the fact that Mr. Joseph Bradford is located at No. 85 Main street, Bulletin Building, for he is a practical blank-book manufacturer, paper ruler and book binder, and is in a position to execute all commissions in a workmanlike, prompt, and generally satisfactory manner. Mr. Bradford was born in Brooklyn, New York, and in 1886 succeeded

B P. LEARNED,

✤ INSURANCE ✤

Office Over Thames National Bank,

Shetucket Street, Norwich, Conn.

It is of course not to be wondered at that the public should give the preference to insurance agencies of long and honorable standing, for no one likes to experiment in insurance matters and there is no inducement to transact business through untried channels as long as tried and approved ones are easily available. For this reason the popularity of the agency conducted by Mr. B. P. Learned, at the Thames Bank building, Shetucket street, is easily accounted for, as the enterprise in question was inaugurated just about forty years ago, and has an enviable record from the very beginning. The founder was Mr. E. Learned, who was succeeded by his son, the present proprietor, in 1866. Mr. B. P. Learned served four years in the army during the Rebellion, and is now well known and popular in Grand Army circles. He represents various leading fire insurance companies and is prepared to write policies on the most favorable terms, his facilities being unsurpassed. Mr. Learned is agent for the largest surety company in the world, AMERICAN SURETY COMPANY, of 160 Broadway, New York. Cash capital, $1,000,000. Those who are required to give bonds in positions of trust, and who desire to avoid asking friends to become their sureties, or who may wish to relieve friends from further obligations as bondsmen, or those who may desire bonds and undertakings required in the courts, should apply in person or by letter to Mr. Learned. He is also agent for the New York Life Insurance Company, and represents the following well-known fire companies: Insurance Company of North America, Philadelphia; Insurance Company, State of Pennsylvania, Philadelphia; Home Insurance Company, New York; Hanover Fire Insurance Company, New York; Citizens Insurance Company, New York; National Fire Insurance Company, Hartford; Lancashire Insurance Company, England; Guardian Assurance Company, London. As may be imagined, Mr. Learned is thoroughly well informed on insurance matters, and he will cheerfully give any desired information on application. A specialty of this agency is the insurance of securities, money, and other valuables by registered mail, which system is being largely used by bankers and other shippers, the rates being much more favorable than those of the express companies with equal security.

The Chelsea Savings Bank, Norwich.—There are few institutions which commend themselves more heartily to the respect of the community than a well managed savings bank, and the history of the Chelsea Savings Bank, during its existence of nearly one third of a century is one in which its founders and managers and the community at large may feel an honest pride. There are enterprises which seem highly beneficial at the outset, but which eventually prove to be unworthy of support ; there are others which fail to develop their innate capacity for usefulness, but so far is this from being the case with the institution in question that we doubt if its founders ever anticipated the full measure of good it has worked in the community. Wage earners have been encouraged to save a portion of their money; the virtues of frugality and economy have been inculcated by practical example, and thousands of dollars' worth of wealth is now in existence which owes its being to the operations of this bank. He who makes two blades of grass grow where one grew before is said to be a public benefactor:—surely an institution which steadily and largely adds to the public wealth is deserving of a similar title. The Chelsea Savings Bank was incorporated in May, 1858, and perhaps the most significant indication of the degree of confidence now reposed in it by the general public is that afforded by the fact that deposits amounting to $4,342,720 70 were held March 1, 1890. This enormous sum of money belongs to a great many individuals, for the bank is conducted in the interests of the people rather than of capitalists, and the average individual holdings are but about $727. Dividends are payable in March and September, and the bank hours are from 10 A. M to 1 P. M. and from 2 to 3 P. M. daily except Saturdays, when the bank closes at noon. The financial condition of the bank is shown by the following statement of March 1, 1890:

LIABILITIES:

Deposits...............................$4,342,720 70
Surplus...............................150,000 00
Profit and Loss.......................79,929 57

Total...............................$4,572,650 27

ASSETS:

Loans on Real Estate...............................$1,257,519 00
Loans to Cities and Towns..........................45,796 00
Loans on Personal Security.........................8,700 00
Loans on Collateral................................699,600 00
United States Bonds................................100,000 00
State Bonds..60,000 00
Municipal Bonds....................................867,000 00
Railroad Bonds.....................................1,093,000 00
Bank Stocks..91,300 00
Real Estate by Foreclosure.........................179,494 67
Banking House......................................23,150 00
Insurance and Taxes................................1,267 17
Cash in Bank.......................................137,085 24
Cash on Hand.......................................8,638 19

Total...............................$4,572,650 27

When it is considered that all the stocks and bonds owned by the bank are held on its books only at par, though the market value is much more, the strength of the bank will be more fully appreciated. The following are the officers of the bank:

President: Henry Bill.
Vice-Presidents: John T. Wait, James A. Hovey, Edward Harland.
Directors: John P. Barstow, O. J. Lamb, Oliver P. Avery, George D Coit, Henry H. Gallup, David A. Billings, William A. Slater, William N. Blackstone, John C. Averill.
Counsel: Jeremiah Halsey.
Attorney: Charles F. Thayer.
Secretary and Treasurer: George D Colt.
Assistant Treasurer: Charles B. Chapman.

Mrs. E. K. Reynolds, Crockery, China, Glassware, Lamp Goods, etc., 159 Main and 17 Shetucket Streets, Norwich, Conn.—All of us cannot be collectors of antique, curious, or artistic china and crockery ware, for this pursuit is a very expensive one and can be followed only by the very rich, but all of us can at least use as beautiful crockery ware in our homes as our circumstances will permit, and it may be said that nowadays a little money will go a great ways in purchasing goods of this kind. Should any of our readers doubt this we will simply refer them to the establishment conducted by Mrs. E. K. Reynolds, at No. 159 Main and No. 17 Shetucket streets, for here may be found an immense and tastefully chosen assortment of crockery, china, glassware, lamp goods, etc., and the prices are certainly low enough to suit the most economically disposed. The premises comprise one floor and a basement, of the dimensions of 60×30 feet, and the heavy stock is arranged to such excellent advantage that examination is easy and pleasant. Employment is given to from three to five assistants, and goods are cheerfully shown at any time, every caller being assured prompt and polite attention. This enterprise was inaugurated in 1877 by Mr. E. K. Reynolds, who was succeeded in 1884 by Mr. J. H. Edwards, Mrs. E. K. Reynolds assuming control in 1886. A very large business is done and the patronage is steadily increasing, both wholesale and retail orders being filled at short notice and at bottom rates.

O. H. Tubbs, Fruits, Candy and Cigars, 225 Main Street, Norwich.—The residents of Norwich and vicinity must be very fond of confectionery and fruits for there is an enormous consumption of these articles, and what is even more significant, this consumption is increasing much faster than the increase in population. Well, provided the public be furnished with honest goods there is nothing to be sorry about, for describe the position taken by a few "cranks" there is no doubt but that candies and fruits are as wholesome as they are delicious. As for obtaining honest goods that is no difficult matter in this city, and no surer way of doing it can possibly be found than that of placing orders with Mr. O. H. Tubbs, as his prices are as reasonable as his goods are acceptable. Mr. Tubbs is a native of this State and has been connected with his present line of business since about 1848. His stock comprises fruits, confectionery, cigars, game in season, etc., and it seems as though all tastes could easily be suited. A fine stock of imported canary birds is carried; also bird cages, seed, and everything in this line. The store is located at No. 225 Main street, and is popular not alone on account of the excellence of the goods and the lowness of the prices, but also by reason of the prompt and courteous attention extended to every caller.

C. W. Barnes, Grocer, 45 Main Street, Preston, Conn.—After visiting the store carried on by Mr. C. W. Barnes, at No. 45 Main street, it is easy to see why the establishment is very popular among all classes of purchasers, for it becomes evident on examination that the stock on hand is very carefully selected and comprises a full line of choice family groceries, and the prices quoted confirm the favorable impression previously made. Mr. Barnes certainly ought to know pretty well what the Preston public wants, for he has been connected with his present business for the past twenty years, having established it in 1870. The premises utilized are 80 × 35 feet in dimensions, and are supplied with all necessary facilities for the accommodation of the stock and the serving of customers promptly and accurately. Teas, coffees and spices are given particular attention and are offered in a variety of choice grades, at exceptionally low rates, while all the many articles dealt in are fully guaranteed to prove as represented and are supplied at prices as low as the lowest. Three competent assistants are employed and all orders are accurately and promptly delivered. Mr. Barnes is a native of Norwich. He has held many public offices in this community, such as selectman, representative, town treasurer and senator.

VOLUNTEER.

Combination Heating Company, Norwich, Ct.—This little portable boiler is especially designed for heating offices, conservatories and small cottage houses. It has a fifteen inch firepot and the Smyth Patent Triangular Grate. It will carry 150 feet of direct steam radiators. The heaters produced by this company have an unsurpassed reputation for efficiency, and are also fully equal to the best as regards durability, and economy of maintenance. Steam heating apparatus is becoming more widely popular every year, and it is apparently only a question of time when the large majority of private residences as well as all public buildings will be equipped with it.

H. D. Rallion, dealer in Choice Family and Fancy Groceries, wholesale and retail, 10 Broadway, Norwich, Conn. —The number of articles which can properly be included under the head "staple and fancy groceries" is increasing every year, and the consequence is that the dealer who really carries a full assortment of them has to keep an extensive and extremely varied stock, and to exercise constant care to see that it is kept complete in every department. As a matter of fact, there are comparatively few who do carry a full assortment, and among these, prominent and favorable mention must be made of Mr. H. D. Rallion, for this gentleman is a representative wholesaler and retailer of groceries, and offers customers a remarkably heavy and desirable stock to choose from. He is a native of Massachusetts and has been identified with his present enterprise since 1884. Very spacious premises are occupied at No. 10 Broadway and employment is given to some half a dozen efficient assistants, goods being delivered to any part of the city and all orders whether large or small being assured prompt and painstaking attention. The stock is far too large and varied to describe in detail in these columns, but we may refer at least to the exceptional inducements offered in the line of canned goods, comprising meats, fish, fruit, vegetables, soups, etc., put up by the leading packers of the world. Sauces, preserves, jellies, and other relishes are also largely handled, together with sugars, coffees, teas, spices, soaps, fruits, vegetables, wood and willow ware, flour, etc., etc. Every article bought of Mr. Rallion is warranted to prove as represented, and is supplied at the lowest market rates in every instance.

Mrs. S. A. Chapman, dealer in Bread, Cake and Pastry, 7 North Thames Street near West Main, Norwich.—We are desirous of calling the attention of our renders to the well known bakery located on Thames street, near West Main street, Norwich, which has been from its inception successful in building up an extensive trade in bread, cake and pastry. This establishment was started fifteen years ago by Mrs. S. A. Chapman, at its present location. The premises are fully equipped with all the necessary requirements for the successful conduct of the business, the extent of which gives employment to thoroughly experienced assistants. Mrs. Chapman carries a fine stock in all branches of her business, and is prepared to supply customers at short notice, with any goods in her line, and perfect satisfaction is guaranteed as to both quality and price. This establishment is largely patronized by families throughout the city, who appreciate first-class bread, cake and pastry of all kinds. Mrs. Chapman is well known throughout Norwich and vicinity. She is a lady of excellent business qualifications, and in her special line offers inducements to purchasers not easily duplicated.

Andrew Millea, Merchant Tailor. Suits Cut and Made in the Latest Style and Warranted to Fit. Also Shirt Patterns Cut. 43 Main Street, Norwich, Conn.—The idea that economy consists of paying as low a price as possible for everything that is purchased is a very mistaken one, and there are few who have had any experience in buying who entertain it. There are many other things to be taken into consideration besides the first cost, especially in the buying of clothing, for in the selection of garments, style, neatness and durability should all be provided for. There are some few who can get a good fit in ready-made clothing and are perfectly satisfied with such garments, but the large majority would have their clothing made to order if they thought they could afford it, and we are convinced that more can afford it than now believe they can, for as a call at the store of Mr. Andrew Millea will prove, first-class custom clothing can now be obtained at but little more than is asked for dependable ready-made garments and the superior wearing qualities of the former more than compensate for the slight difference in price. Mr. Millea has carried on his present business since 1868 and should certainly be in a position to satisfy the most critical both as regards price and workmanship. He carries a fine and varied stock of foreign and domestic fabrics, and a visit to his establishment, No. 43 Main street, will show that all tastes and ages can be suited. A perfect fit is guaranteed and every garment is cut in the very latest style. Shirt patterns also are cut here, and as employment is given to six competent assistants all orders are assured immediate and satisfactory attention and can be delivered at short notice.

J. E. Hawkins, dealer in Hats, Caps, Furs and Gentlemen's Furnishing Goods, sole Agent for Dunlap's Celebrated Fifth Avenue Hats. 146 Main Street, Norwich, Conn. —Theory and practice are supposed to agree of course, but it is notorious that they sometimes diverge in a most singular and noticeable manner. In theory, every dealer in certain goods in a certain community should have to sell at uniform rates, as otherwise those who charged the higher prices would do no business at all, but in practice all of us know that such is far from being the case. Probably in no line of business is this more noticeable than in that devoted to the sale of hats, furnishings, etc., for precisely similar goods are sold at greatly varying prices by different dealers. Of course the wise man buys where he can get the most for his money, and in this connection we may fittingly call attention to the establishment conducted by J. E. Hawkins, successor to Frink & Main, at No. 146 Main street, for here are quoted prices as low as the lowest, on goods that will surely give entire satisfaction. This enterprise was started about forty years ago, and came under the control of the present proprietor in 1889. He caters to all classes of trade, carries a very extensive and varied stock of hats, caps, gloves, and men's furnishings in general, handles the very latest fashionable novelties and guarantees every article sold to prove precisely as represented.

LEADING BUSINESS MEN OF NORWICH.

J. B. Merrow & Sons, makers of the Merrow Special Crochet Machine, 18 and 20 White's Court, Norwich.—

Such wonderful progress has been made within the past half century in the invention and introduction of machinery, that it would be a rash or an ignorant man who would set bounds to possible achievement in this direction. We often hear a machine referred to as doing its work with "human accuracy," but as a matter of fact, "human accuracy" is far exceeded by some of the more perfect appliances now in everyday use, and they make results possible which would be quite out of the question under different conditions. One of the most original, efficient and useful pieces of apparatus which has been put on the market for years is the Merrow Special Crochet Machine, which is designed to be used for finishing knit goods, and which does its work with an ease and rapidity which are really marvelous when the difficulties to be overcome are considered. We will attempt no description of this machine; first, because verbal descriptions of machinery convey no ideas whatever, unless phrased in technical language and addressed to trained mechanics; and second because such of our readers as are sufficiently interested have only to call at the factory where this machine is made, Nos. 18 and 20 White's Court, or to communicate with the makers, Messrs. J. B. Merrow & Sons, in order to be put in the way of becoming thoroughly familiar with the appliance as it appears in practical operation. The machine will finish the edges of all knit goods, from the finest to the heaviest, and is so rapid, simple and satisfactory in operation as to commend itself on sight to every practical man. In these days of sharp competition, any machine that will tend to reduce the cost of production is of vital interest to manufacturers, and it is safe to assert that the advantages gained by the use of this machine are marvelous. The mechanical construction of the machine is worthy of the reputation of its makers, it being manufactured from carefully selected material by skilled workmen, aided by the latest improved machinery. Every machine leaving the factory is guaranteed to be as represented and perfect in all its parts. Messrs. J. B Merrow & Sons are prepared to fill the largest orders at short notice and will be happy to give information on application.

Bisket & Meech, Pharmacists, corner Main and Sixth Streets, Norwich, Conn.—The pharmacy carried on by Messrs. Bisket & Meech, at the corner of Main and Sixth streets was established in 1876, by Mr. Bisket, the present firm having been formed in 1878. This establishment has long ranked among the representative ones of the kind in this portion of the State. Mr. Bisket is a native of Scotland, and Mr. Meech of Southbridge, Mass. They are both members of the Odd Fellows ; Mr. Bisket is also connected with the Knights of Pythias, and Mr. Meech with the Red Men. Much of the success they have attained in building up a large and desirable trade is due to their habit of giving close personal attention to the many details

of their business. The premises made use of are 55 × 20 feet in dimensions, and are excellently fitted up for the purposes to which they are devoted. A heavy and complete stock is at all times carried, comprising drugs, medicines and chemicals in great variety, the goods being obtained from the leading producers and wholesalers, and being fully up to the highest standard in every respect. Prescriptions are compounded in the most methodical and skillful manner, no pains being spared to ensure absolute accuracy in even the most trivial details.

A. B. KINGSBURY,
JEWELER.
Watches, Clocks and Silver Ware.
172 Main Street, Norwich.

Norwich Lock Mfg. Co., manufacturers of Locks, Knobs, and Builders' Hardware, Norwich, Conn.—The business conducted by the Norwich Lock Manufacturing Company was founded in 1865, and for some time was carried on by the Norwich Lock Company, the present corporation having been organized in 1872. This is one of the largest concerns in the United States engaged in the manufacture of locks, padlocks and builders' hardware. An idea of the popularity of these goods is to investigate the facilities for their production, and certainly it is obvious that the demand for them must be immense when it is necessary to employ 250 assistants, aided by the most efficient machinery obtainable, in order to fill the orders received. Motive power is furnished by an eighty-horse engine, and the premises utilized include a foundry of the dimensions of 200 × 50 feet, a factory three stories in height and 150 × 50 feet in size, and other smaller buildings. The capacity of the works is 300 dozen locks, an equal number of knobs, and various specialties in builders' hardware daily, and immense as this capacity is it is often none too great to properly supply the demand. The company has a capital of $75,000 and its business is largely increasing every year. The president is Mr. H H. O-good, and the secretary and treasurer is Mr. Charles H Beebe ; these gentlemen being associated on the board of directors with Messrs. Sidney Turner, E. N. Gibbs and Charles A. Converse.

George A. Lewis, dealer in Fancy Groceries, Fruit and Oysters, Ice Cream at wholesale and retail, Corner Central Avenue and Fourth Street, Norwich, Conn.—As fine an example of a business enterprise, having a gradual and extensive growth, as we know of in this vicinity, is that afforded by the undertaking conducted by Mr. George A. Lewis. This gentleman ranks with the leading dealers of fancy groceries, fruit and oysters in Greeneville, and has gained his present position from small beginnings, the enterprise being inaugurated in 1885. The premises utilized are located at the corner of Central avenue and Fourth street, and comprise one floor 40×35 feet in dimensions, being admirably adapted to the handling of the varied stock dealt in, which comprises in addition to fancy groceries, fruits and oysters, and ice cream, which is sold at both wholesale and retail. Two competent assistants are employed, and the enterprising business methods pursued puts the proprietor in a position to successfully meet all competition and push his specialties with vigor, and to the complete satisfaction of customers. Mr. Lewis is a native of Lisbon, Conn, and is well known in this community and bears an honorable and enviable reputation for the invariable employment of strictly legitimate business methods, as well as the accuracy and promptitude with which orders entrusted to him are filled.

A. T. Otis, dealer in Groceries, Provisions, etc., 261 Main Street, Norwich, Conn.—It is no discredit to the other excellent grocery and provision stores in Norwich to say that that carried on by Mr. A. T. Otis has hardly its rival in town, for this business was founded fully half a century ago, and so long a "start" is not easily to be made up by competitors. The present proprietor has had control for more than a quarter of a century, or since 1864, and considering the present status of the enterprise, it is hardly necessary to say that he has never depended upon the past prestige of the establishment but has spared no pains to meet all honorable competition, the result being a general knowledge on the part of the public that in no store in the county can a dollar be spent to more advantage in the purchase of dependable family food supplies. The premises made use of comprise one floor and a basement of the dimensions of 65×30 feet, and are conveniently located at No. 261 Main street. Employment is given to three experienced and careful assistants, and orders will be accurately filled and delivered at short notice. The stock comprises staple and fancy groceries in almost endless variety, obtained from the most reputable sources, and admirably adapted to the requirements of the most select trade, while no exorbitant prices are quoted in any department, the lowest market rates being closely adhered to.

Miss E. Congdon, Ladies' and Gents' Restaurant. Meals Served at All Hours. No. 6 Franklin street, Norwich, Conn —One of the mysteries of life in our American cities has always been the poorness of the restaurant facilities. It is not so in other countries—in England, Germany or France—for in all of those nations may be found many excellent public eating houses where good meals may be obtained at moderate expense, but in the United States it is really difficult to find a well-managed and moderate-priced restaurant. We therefore take all the more pleasure in calling attention to that carried on by Miss E. Congdon, at No. 6 Franklin street, for this is an establishment which can be unhesitatingly commended to all who appreciate carefully selected and well cooked food, prompt and polite service, and uniformly reasonable prices. The premises made use of are of the dimensions of 60×30 feet and are very neatly and conveniently fitted up. Employment is given to four assistants, and meals are promptly and politely served at all hours. Miss Congdon began operations here in 1886, and is to be congratulated on her success in building up her present extensive and steadily increasing business. She gives it close personal supervision and is constantly striving to improve the service rendered, while her prices will compare very favorably with those demanded at many other establishments offering decidedly inferior accommodations.

J. C. Monroe, Blacksmith Shop, Central Wharf, Norwich, Conn.—Mr. J. C. Monroe is a native of Norwich, and has long been prominently identified with the blacksmith's trade, being known as one of the most expert blacksmiths in the city. Since he opened his new shop, on Central Wharf, in rear of C. B. Rogers' foundry, he has materially added to both his reputation and his business, for his improved facilities enable him to fill every order without long delay and to do work cheaply as well as durably and neatly. The premises made use of are 65×35 feet in dimensions and are thoroughly equipped in every part, especially as regards the facilities for heavy work, of which a specialty is made. All kinds of carriage ironing and woodwork are done in a superior manner at short notice, employment being given to from two to three competent assistants. Mr. Monroe gives particular attention to the shoeing of horses and is prepared to do such work in a manner that will suit customers, no rigid rules being followed but the individual needs of each horse being carefully considered. The prices quoted in the various departments of the business are as low as is consistent with the use of selected material and the employment of skilled labor, and we may say in closing that all work done at this establishment is fully warranted in every respect.

Ansel Clark, Contractor and Builder, wholesale and retail dealer in Stone, Brick, Slate, Cement, Lime, Hair, Plaster, Fire Brick, Fire Clay, Beach Sand, Drain Pipe, Sheathing Paper (Dry and Tarred); Marble and Slate Mantles, and Center Pieces. Prompt attention given to orders for Mason Work of all descriptions, and Slate Roofing. Manufacturer of the Avery Low Pressure Improved Steam Heater, 13 Water Street, Norwich, Conn. —It is of the very highest importance to have mason work

properly done in the first place, for alterations and repairs are bound to be expensive and it is obvious that the stability of a house with the experience of that of Ansel Clark assures the best of work in every department of the business. During the more than half a century that he has carried on his present business he has established a wide-spread reputation for skill and thoroughness. He was born in Hebron, Conn., and came to Norwich in 1836, beginning business as a member of the firm of Leonard & Clark and assuming sole control in 1859. Mr. Clark has been connected with the city government and is almost universally known hereabouts. He is a contractor and builder who is in a position to figure very closely on specifications, and those contemplating building would best serve their own interests by communicating with him. Mr. Clark is also manufacturer of the Avery Low Pressure Improved Steam Heater, which fully solves the problem of steam-heating without the least danger and is remarkably economical and efficient. The premises utilized are located at No. 13 Water street, and comprise two floors measuring 55 × 25 feet, together with sheds, wharf room, etc., for a very heavy and varied stock is carried, Mr. Clark being an extensive wholesale and retail dealer in stone, brick, slate; Roman, Portland and Rosendale cement; lime for all purposes, hair, plaster, fire-brick, fire-clay, beach sand, drain pipe, dry and tarred sheathing paper, marble and slate mantels and centre pieces, etc. The office has telephone connection and orders are acted upon without delay.

W. H. Vincent, manufacturer, jobber and retailer of Fine Confectionery, No. 58 Broadway, Norwich, Conn.—There is no doubt but that the consumption of confectionery is steadily increasing, even faster than the increase in population, but it is equally unquestionable that this increased demand is for goods of superior merit and not for the "grocer's candies," which were at one time so popular. The fact is, not only are the people getting richer and hence having more money to spend on luxuries, but the standard of taste is being raised, and choicer and more delicately flavored candies are being demanded annually. Mr. W. H. Vincent of No. 58 Broadway, has built up a very large and desirable trade during the comparatively short time that he has conducted his present establishment, and this success is the natural consequence of his recognizing the facts to which we have referred. He at all times carries a large and varied stock, and spares no pains to offer goods that will surely suit the most fastidious, Mr. Vincent is most excellently prepared to do this, as he is a manufacturer as well as a jobber and retailer and hence knows just what he is furnishing to his patrons. The premises utilized are 55 × 18 feet in dimensions and are tastefully and conveniently fitted up, the stock being displayed to excellent advantage and being renewed so frequently that the goods comprising it are always fresh and attractive. The lowest market rates are quoted both on wholesale and retail orders, and every article sold by Mr. Vincent is guaranteed to prove precisely as represented.

Louis Salomon, dealer in Clothing and Gents' Furnishing, Trunks, Valises, etc., etc.. No. 29 Shetucket Street. Norwich, Conn.—An experienced and discriminating buyer can obtain clothing and gentlemen's furnishings nowadays at very low rates, for clothing is cheaper to-day probably than it ever was before, and one only has to patronize the right establishments in order to get a good deal of value for a very little money. But it may be asked, "whose are the right establishments?" These are not hard to find for one who will use his eyes, his ears, and his commonsense, and as good a one as can be named is that conducted by Mr. Louis Salomon at No. 29 Shetucket street. This gentleman was born in Germany, and has carried on his present enterprise since 1878, during which time he has built up an enviable reputation for handling dependable goods, quoting bottom prices, and extending equally prompt and courteous attention to large and small buyers. The store is 75 × 30 feet in dimensions and at all times contains a large and carefully chosen stock of clothing, gentlemen's furnishings, trunks, bags, valises, etc., the latest fashionable novelties being represented and a sufficient variety being at hand to enable all tastes and purses to be suited. Employment is given to two experienced and polite assistants, and goods will be cheerfully shown at any time. Mr. Salomon does an extensive business, and certainly no one can begrudge success so honestly and thoroughly deserved.

Henry B. Gray, Livery, Boarding and Sale Stables Nos. 8-12 Bath Street, Norwich.—The premises utilized by Mr. Henry B. Gray have been used for stable purposes for many years, these stables ranking with the oldest established in the city. They came into the possession of the present proprietor in 1884, and it is but fair to say have not only maintained but largely increased their popularity under his liberal and skilful management. Mr. Gray was born in Ledyard, Conn., and has a very large circle of friends in Norwich and vicinity. He has from the very first made a practice of using his customers well, and as a natural consequence his reputation for fair dealing is of the very best. The premises made use of comprise two floors of the dimensions of 100 × 60 feet, and are very conveniently fitted up. Mr. Gray does an extensive livery, boarding and sale business, and employs three competent assistants. He is prepared to furnish first-class single or double teams at very short notice, and at rates that can but prove entirely satisfactory to every reasonable patron. Horses boarded here are assured the best of care and an abundance of suitable food, while the stalls are roomy and well ventilated. Special accommodations are provided for those wishing to bait their horses, and a fine office is at the disposal of ladies wishing to leave bundles or to wait for their team. The stable is also centrally located near the principal stores and banks. Mr. Gray often has some very desirable animals to sell, and those who are looking for a good roadster and can appreciate the advantages gained by buying of a perfectly responsible party would do well to give him a call.

J. P. Holloway, dealer in Fine Groceries, Flour, Tea, etc., 267 Main Street, Norwich, Conn.—The business conducted by Mr. J. P. Holloway at No. 267 Main street, was founded about 1874 by Mr. J. F. Crittenden, and in 1879 came into the possession of Messrs. Holloway Bros., this firm being composed of Messrs. G. A. and J. P. Holloway. The former gentleman retired in February, 1886, since which date the present proprietor has had sole control. He is a native of Groton, and has a very large circle of friends throughout Norwich and vicinity. The business has developed greatly since its inception, and now requires the employment of two competent assistants and the carrying of a heavy and varied stock, comprising fine groceries, flour, tea, coffees, canned goods, etc., etc. Premises of the dimensions of 60×30 feet are occupied and the goods are displayed to excellent advantage, the store being neat and trim and supplied with all necessary facilities for the storage and handling of the commodities dealt in. Mr. Holloway is in a position to meet all honorable competition, and his prices will be found to bear the closest comparison with those quoted elsewhere on goods of equal merit. Making a specialty of family trade, he spares no pains to handle reliable articles only, and customers appreciate this fact and know that all goods coming from his store are sure to prove precisely as represented.

M. Hourigan, Undertaker and dealer in Furniture, Carpets, Oil Cloths, Wall Papers, Coffins, Caskets, Robes, etc., 66 Main Street, Norwich, Conn.—It is undoubtedly true that house furnishing goods are cheaper to-day than they ever were before and that about every man can now afford to furnish his home comfortably and even handsomely, but it is also true that many practically worthless goods are in the market and that the only safe course to take is to place orders with a dealer who has proved himself to be worthy of every confidence. In this connection we may very properly call attention to the establishment conducted by Mr. M. Hourigan, at No. 66 Main street, for here may be found a large and exceptionally complete stock of furniture, carpets, oil cloths, wall papers and general house furnishings, and during the score of years that Mr. Hourigan has carried on this business he has attained a well-deserved reputation for representing things just as they are and for quoting the lowest market rates in every department of his business. Operations were begun by him in 1869, and the enterprise afterwards came under the control of Messrs. Hourigan & Doyle the present owner resuming sole possession in 1878. The premises utilized comprise two floors, measuring 85×45 feet, and employment is given to three competent assistants, no pains being spared to assure immediate as well as polite attention to every caller. Mr. Hourigan does an extensive undertaking business and constantly carries a complete stock of coffins, caskets, robes and funeral goods in general. Orders are acted upon without delay and moderate charges are made under all circumstances.

O. L. Offenheiser, wholesale dealer in Foreign and Domestic Fruit of all kinds; Post-office Box, 1142; 42 Market Street, Norwich, Conn.—Fruit has been called "the only perfect food with the exception of milk," and there is no doubt whatever but that the judicious eating of fruit will do much to fortify the system against disease by promoting digestion and otherwise assisting the various processes incidental to the maintenance of life. The United States has long been known as "a nation of dyspeptics," but if fruit continues to gain here in popularity, this term will soon be no longer applicable. Both foreign and domestic fruits may now be had at a very low price, for steam and enterprise have worked wonders, and the productions of tropical countries and of the southern portion of our own country are now offered in the northern markets at rates within the means of all. One of the leading wholesale dealers in foreign and domestic fruit, doing business in this section, is Mr. C. L. Offenheiser, located at No. 42 Market street. This gentleman is a native of New York City, and has been identified with his present establishment since 1885. He handles all kinds of fruit, and employs three competent assistants. Mr. Offenheiser is in a position to fill the heaviest orders at short notice, and to quote positively bottom prices at all times. Communications addressed to P. O. Box, 1142, will receive immediate and careful attention, and retailers would do well to look into the advantages that Mr. Offenheiser is prepared to offer.

Richard F. Goodwin, successor to Goodwin & Parker, manufacturers of Machine Cut Corks, 93 and 95 Chestnut Street, Norwich, Conn.—Perhaps some of our readers may have been curious at one time or another to know where all the corks come from, for it is obvious that an immense number must be manufactured in order to satisfy the extensive and constantly increasing demand for them. One of the largest manufacturers of corks in eastern Connecticut is Mr. Richard F. Goodwin and his factory is a very instructive place to visit for those who are interested in the subject, for it contains a complete plant of improved machinery which is capable of turning out machine-cut corks, granulated corks, seine corks, cork washers and sliced cork, with a rapidity and accuracy which are fairly amazing. This business was founded in 1867 by Messrs. Goodwin & Parker, and has been under the sole control of the present proprietor since 1884. The premises made use of comprise two floors of the dimensions of 90×50 feet, and are supplied with steam power, some twenty horse-power being required to drive the machinery in use. Mr. Goodwin deals largely in corks for all bottling purposes and makes it a rule to keep a full line of such constantly on hand. He also deals in hand corking machines, and makes a specialty of cork washers and sliced cork, being prepared to fill the most extensive orders for these or in fact for anything in his line, without delay and at prices in strict accordance with the lowest market rates.

Fellows & Rice, Masons and Builders, Plain and Ornamental Plasterers; dealers in Brick Lime, Cement, Hair, Sand, Marble and Slate Mantels and Center Pieces, Brackets and Ornaments, 149 and 151 Water Street, Norwich, Conn.—The firm of Fellows & Rice was formed in 1885, and it is safe to say that the reputation since built up is second to that of no concern in a similar line of business in the city. Messrs. Fellows & Rice are masons and builders, plain and ornamental plasterers and dealers in brick, lime, cement, sand, hair, etc., as well as marble and slate mantels, center pieces, brackets and ornaments. The premises made use of comprise two floors of the dimensions of 70 × 25 feet, and employment is given to fifteen competent and careful assistants, so that all orders can be filled without undue delay and in an entirely satisfactory manner. Mr. G. E. Fellows was born in New London, and Mr. F. G. Rice in this city, both these gentlemen being very thoroughly acquainted with the practical details of their business. Particular attention is paid to

orders for mason work of all kinds and as estimates will be cheerfully and promptly made on application, those contemplating building should by all means give this representative firm an opportunity to bid. Slate roofing is also done in a superior manner at short notice, and the charges made in every department of the business will be found to be moderate and fair in every instance.

James Murphy, dealer in Groceries and Provisions, Fine Wines, Liquors, Ales, Cigars and Tobacco, 3 Water Street, Norwich, Conn.—The business of which Mr. James Murphy is proprietor was founded by him just about ten years ago and has steadily developed until it has reached quite extensive proportions. He is a dealer in groceries and provisions of all descriptions, and also handles fine wines, liquors, ales, cigars and tobacco, being well prepared to furnish first-class goods at reasonable prices. The premises utilized have an area of 1500 square feet and are very conveniently fitted up, enabling orders to be filled at short notice and in a thoroughly accurate and satisfactory manner. The stock is so uniformly good that it is difficult to single out certain articles for individual mention, but we may at least call attention to the assortment of teas, coffees and spices, these being of standard purity, of fine and delicate flavor and of comparatively low cost. Fresh vegetables and other country produce are also always well represented in the stock, and those who appreciate good butter and cheese should most certainly test the goods offered by Mr. Murphy at No. 3 Water street. Pure liquors for medicinal and family use are a leading specialty, and will be supplied in quantities to suit at low figures.

C. W. Perkins, Carpenter, Builder and General Jobber. Orders promptly attended to; Office, Central Wharf, 65 W. Main Street, opposite Edw. Chappell & Co., Norwich.— Mr. C. W. Perkins is a native of Norwich, and has carried on his present enterprise since 1885, during which time he has attained an enviable reputation for filling orders at short notice, at moderate rates and in a thoroughly workmanlike manner. He is in a position to figure very closely on plans and specifications, and those who propose to do any building should most certainly give him a chance to estimate as to the cost of the work, for such estimates will be promptly and cheerfully furnished and one may save money, time and trouble by submitting his plans to Mr. Perkins. There is one decided advantage in placing orders with him and that is the certainty that every agreement made concerning the work will be carefully respected and fully carried out. This assurance entirely obviates the anxiety which is sure to result from the awarding of a contract to a less dependable builder, and even if Mr. Perkins were not prepared to make bottom figures it would still be worth while to take advantage of the facilities he offers. Employment is given to four or more assistants, according to the season, etc., and as care is taken to hire reliable help only, the results attained are sure to be entirely satisfactory.

C. W. Hill, Grocer, 19 Franklin Square, Norwich, Conn. —Among those grocery and ten houses which, both on account of the character and extent of the stock carried and the low prices named on the articles comprising the same, are worthy of especially prominent and favorable mention, must be classed that conducted by Mr. C. W. Hill on Franklin square, for this gentleman caters to the most fastidious trade, while his prices are as low as the lowest in every department, quality of course being considered. The premises are of spacious dimensions, and afford ample accommodations for the heavy assortment of choice flour, staple and fancy groceries, teas, coffees and spices, which is constantly carried. A full selection of everything usually carried in a first-class grocery store is always to be found here. Employment is given to thoroughly experienced assistants, and orders will be promptly and courteously filled at all times. Mr. Hill gives the details of his business careful personal supervision and spares no pains to assure complete satisfaction to the most critical customers.

A. F. Howard, Dentist, 197 Main Street (over Boston Store), Norwich, Conn.—This is neither the time nor the place to discuss the causes of defective teeth, but it is generally believed that the unenviable distinction possessed by the Americans of having the poorest teeth of any nation, is the consequence of a combination of hereditary influences, bad habits of eating, improper selection of food and unpardonable carelessness in caring for the teeth. Of late years there has been a sort of hygienic "revival," which has undoubtedly accomplished great good already and is sure to continue to spread that knowledge of the prime laws of health which is essential to the physical well-being of a community. If Americans have the worst teeth in the world, they have the best dentists, and so true is this and so generally conceded and widely known, that foreigners come here to study dentistry as we send our sons abroad to finish their education in medicine or in art. Where the standard is so high it is of course difficult to gain an exceptional reputation, and yet we believe that Dr. A. F. Howard, of No. 197 Main street, fully deserves the reputation he holds for superior skill and gentleness. At all events, we know that those who have availed themselves of his services speak in the highest terms of the methods he employs, and certainly they should be in a position to render intelligent and convincing judgment. Dr. Howard was born in New York City, and succeeded Dr. G. G. Bishop here in Norwich in 1885. He utilizes two good-sized apartments—a thoroughly equipped operating room and an elegantly furnished reception room—and has every facility at his hand for the practice of dentistry in all its branches in accordance with the most approved methods. All work is fully guaranteed, and the scale of prices is moderate and satisfactory.

J. C. Worth, wholesale Commission Merchant in Foreign and Domestic Fruits and Vegetables ; Strawberries and Peaches a specialty in their season ; 34 and 36 Market Street, Norwich, Conn.—The development of the trade in foreign and domestic fruits has been one of the most remarkable commercial changes occurring of late years, for although foreign fruits have long been a staple commodity in the market, still it is only recently that their handling has engaged the attention of men of such energy and such capital as to have caused imported fruits to retail as low, and in some cases lower, than fruits raised right here in the North. One of the men most prominently identified with the handling of foreign and domestic fruits and vegetables in this vicinity, is Mr. J. C. Worth, doing business at Nos. 34 and 36 Market street. This gentleman is a native of Fayal, Azore Islands, and began operations in 1873, as a member of the firm of J. C. Worth & Co., assuming sole control in 1884. He does a wholesale commission business and utilizes two floors, each of which measures 45 × 30 feet. Mr. Worth makes a specialty of strawberries and peaches in their season ; and at all times carries a large and seasonable stock. His store has telephone connection, and orders are assured immediate and careful attention, as employment is given to four competent assistants, and the heaviest commissions can be executed at short notice.

F. L. Gardner, dealer in Fine Groceries and Teas, Provisions, Flour, Grain, Fruit, Wooden Ware, etc., corner Market and Water Streets, Norwich, Conn.—Probably one of the oldest established businesses of the kind in this city is that conducted by Mr. F. L. Gardner at the corner of Market and Water streets, for this enterprise was inaugurated very nearly half a century ago, its inception occurring in 1841. The present proprietor is a native of Norwich and has become thoroughly identified with the undertaking in question, he having carried it on ever since 1869. The premises utilized comprise four floors measuring 15 × 20 feet each, and a heavy stock is constantly on hand to choose from, it being made up of choice staple and fancy groceries, selected teas and coffees, pure spices, flour, grain, fruit, provisions, wooden ware and many

other commodities too numerous to mention. Mr. Gardner employs three competent assistants and is in a position to assure immediate and courteous attention to every caller. He caters to no special class of trade but strives to offer a sufficient variety of goods to suit all tastes and purses, and to quote positively the lowest market rates at all times. He has built up an extensive business during his long and honorable career and has an unsurpassed reputation for selling goods strictly on their merits, no misrepresentation being practiced under any circumstances.

N. D. Lamb, Confectioner and dealer in Toys, Fancy Goods, Fruit, Nuts, etc., 48 Main Street, Norwich, Conn.—There is a great deal of nonsense spoken and written concerning the food we eat and the beverages we drink, and probably what has been said in connection with the use of confectionery contains a greater proportion of nonsense than can be pointed out in any other line. Fortunately the commonsense of the people is not to be easily led astray by even the most ingenious theories of so called "scientists," and therefore the consumption of confectionery has steadily continued to increase despite the frantic efforts of sensationalists and alarmists. It is a noteworthy fact however that the *quality* of the confectionery now in general use is much higher than was the case a decade ago, and the leading confectioners report that the demand for the higher grades of candies is constantly and rapidly increasing. It is largely owing to his appreciation of this fact that Mr. N. D. Lamb has built up so desirable a business since beginning operations in 1874, for he has spared no pains to offer goods that would satisfy the most fastidious, and as a consequence has a select as well as a large circle of patrons. Mr. Lamb was born in Norwich. He does a retail business in confectionery, fruit, toys, etc., and a wholesale business in ice-cream, supplying the latter commodity in any desired quantity and at the lowest market rates. The premises are located at No. 48 Main street, and measure 45 × 30 feet, a portion of them being tastefully fitted up as an ice-cream saloon. A fine stock of doll carriages, toys, fancy goods, etc., etc , is handled. Patrons are assured prompt and courteous attention, and no better candy or ice-cream is obtainable in this city.

J. P. Collins & Co., manufacturers of Collins' Improved Jouval Turbine, with First Transmitting Machinery, Norwich, Conn —The many and valuable water privileges to be found in New England were of course what gave that section its prominence as a manufacturing section, and the only way in which this prominence can be maintained is by the proper utilization of the local water powers. Steam has, of course, worked great changes in manufacturing methods, but water-power—when suitably availed of—is still the most economical power known and this gives its user a decided advantage in the close competition of the present day. Many a mill privilege which is now practically abandoned might be put to practical and profitable use by the employment of Collins's Improved Jouval Turbine, and many a mill which is now only partially run by water-power might dispense with the use of steam altogether were this apparatus introduced. These assertions are not made lightly, for practical experience proves them to be fully justified by the facts. Mr. Collins has devoted himself to the designing and construction of water wheels for many years and is the inventor of a past-gate guide which is acknowledged to be superior to all others, it being the only one which has been applied successfully to the Jouval Turbine. The firm have turned out many wheels during their business career and it is estimated that one fourth of all the cotton spindles in this country run by water power are driven by the Collins Improved Jouval Turbine. Any mill in New England will be visited on application, free of expense, all necessary surveys, etc., being made and estimates furnished. Orders can be filled at comparatively short notice and no pains will be spared to fully maintain the enviable reputation thus far held.

W. W. Sheffield, D. D. S., Harris Building, New London.—Without denying for a moment that artificial teeth on a movable plate are far superior to no teeth at all, it may still be confidently asserted that such teeth are clumsy, uncomfortable, comparatively inefficient, and in short unsatisfactory. The popular prejudice against covering the roof of the mouth with a plate is not at all difficult to understand, and that such a plate impairs the sense of taste is too thoroughly established to admit of successful denial. Various attempts have been made to obviate the necessity for such plates but none of the devices as yet produced have met with even a small proportion of the success attained by those incidental to what is known as Dr. Sheffield's Perfect Crowning System. The merits of this system are established by years of practical experience, for during the past decade more than 30,000 crowns and bridges have been inserted without a single failure. This system consists of the permanent attachment of artificial gold and porcelain-faced crowns to the roots of the natural teeth, and the attachment of artificial teeth to bridges. The fundamental operation on which the lasting success of this system is based, is the treatment and permanent cure of all diseased conditions existing, after which the crown and bridge work may be applied with a certainty of satisfactory results. The inventors, projectors and proprietors of this valuable system are W. W. Sheffield, D. D. S., of this city, and Lucius T. Sheffield, D. M. D., of New York. Dr. W. W. Sheffield is a native of N. Stonington, Conn., and has long been one of the leading dentists of New England. His rooms in the Harris Building are magnificently fitted up, and are among the best equipped in the country. Three operating rooms are available, and seven thoroughly competent assistants are in attendance, for the doctor does an immense business and carries on dentistry in all its branches. He is universally known throughout this section. Dr. Sheffield has made a life-long study of the teeth in health and in disease, and has produced two preparations—" Crème Dentifrice " and " Elixir Balm " which are designed to promote the health of the teeth and gums, perfume the breath and prevent decay. They are sold at a moderate figure, may be used together or separately and are of genuine and decided value, besides being perfectly harmless and far superior to anything else in the market. Can be found at all the druggists.

E. D. Harris, dealer in Anthracite and Bituminous Coal. Offices at 207 Main Street and 449 North Main Street, Norwich, Conn.—The increasing popularity of open fire places is greatly to be commended for it is based on commonsense, although of course, many use this method of heating simply because it is fashionable. We speak of the use of open fire-places as a "method of heating," and so it is, but it is still more a method of ventilation, and one that thus far is without a rival. Not one city house in a hundred is properly ventilated, and several well-placed open fires will do more to change the air and carry off the germs of disease than four times that number of stoves or furnaces. Coal cannot be burned so economically in this way of course, but medicines cost even more than coal, and good health is cheap at any price. In order to get the greatest possible benefit from open fires a superior quality of coal must be used, and as much that is sold for this purpose is quite unsuitable and is apt to prejudice the public against the use of open grates altogether, we take pleasure in calling attention to the coal offered by Mr. E. D. Harris, for he makes a specialty of handling coal adapted to open fires and is prepared to supply a superior article in quantities to suit and at positively the lowest market rates. Mr. Harris is a native of Preston, and began operations in 1884. He has offices at No. 207 Main street, and No. 449 North Main street, and employs ten assistants, all orders large or small being assured immediate and careful attention. The storage facilities available are sufficient to accommodate 5000 tons, and all the standard grades of anthracite and bituminous coal are constantly carried in stock, so that the wants of all classes of consumers can be satisfactorily supplied.

Whaley's Cafe, 6 Shetucket Street, Norwich.—There are not so many first class dining rooms in Norwich as to make such establishments too common to call for particular notice, and indeed this city is not exceptional in this respect for although the United States leads the world in some things, it makes a sorry showing in comparison with other civilized countries as far as public restaurants are concerned. The difficulty of finding an establishment where good food, good cooking and courteous service are assured to every caller, has frequently been referred to by strangers traveling in this country, as well as by native writers, and we will not dwell upon it, preferring the much more pleasant task of informing our readers where a thoroughly satisfactory dining room may be found. " Whaley's Café " is of course well known to many of our readers, but to those who are not familiar with it we have simply to say that its superior is not to be found in this section, as a trial will conclusively prove. Mr. Charles H. Whaley, the proprietor is a native of Hartford, and founded his present business in 1876. He has developed it by giving careful attention to the wants of the public, sparing no pains to provide an efficient, economical and satisfactory service. The bill of fare is varied, and skillfully made up, and the food is of the choicest quality and is very attractively served. Mr. Whaley carries a large stock of baker's goods, fruits, confectionery, cigars, etc., and quotes low prices on all the goods he handles.

O. W. Scott, Jr., successor to B. F. Brewster, Practical Horse-shoer, Shop on Chestnut Street, rear of Broadway Church. Particular attention paid to Shoeing Gentlemen's Driving Horses, Norwich, Conn.—This is a very old stand and was utilized for many years by Mr. B. F. Brewster before the present proprietor assumed control in 1879. It is very thoroughly fitted up, and as employment is given to three efficient assistants the extensive business done can be easily and promptly attended to. Mr Scott gives particular attention to the shoeing of gentlemen's driving horses. A specialty made of all lameness and diseases of foot. Variety of shoes and expanders to rectify the gaits of horses and restore the foot to its natural shape. On account of the demand and beneficial results, we find it necessary to keep all sizes of Dr. Roberge's patent Hoof Expanders in stock. They may be applied by us in all sizes at reasonable terms I have used them for a number of years. I can safely recommend them if properly applied. The peculiarities of each horse are carefully studied and the shoe is made to fit the hoof; the hoof not being pared, burned and hacked away to fit the shoe. No fancy charges are made and we can safely guarantee satisfaction to every customer. Constantly on hand, condition powders, liniment and hoof ointment.

Photographic and Art Studio. Photographs made in Every Style, and all work promptly and satisfactorily finished. Special attention given to large work, such as Crayon, India Ink, Water Colors, or Solar Photographs. Copying done in all its branches. No. 197 Main Street, Williams Block, Norwich, Conn.—An absolutely perfect portrait is rarely produced, either by drawing, painting or photography, and despite the remarkable progress made in the last named profession of late years, it is safe to assert that there are to day more bad than good photographs produced. Not but what the people are capable of discriminating between a good and a bad picture, but because (on account of some curious notions of economy) they put up with an inferior portrait simply because they can get it a little "cheaper." Of course there are thousands who do not allow themselves to be led into this error, but still there are even more who do, and this latter class are the salvation of the many incompetent and careless photographers which are unhappily to be found in this country. The very best portrait, we say, is none too good, and the very best portrait is also the very cheapest, for a poor portrait is certainly not worth bringing home. The difference in price between really artistic and miserably inferior work is after all but trifling, and those who cannot afford to pay this difference would unquestionably adopt the wisest course should they go without any portraits whatever. Believing as we do that in photography even more than in anything else "the best is cheapest," it is natural that we should cordially recommend to our readers the establishment conducted by Mr. J. O. Durgan at No. 197 Main street, Williams' Block, for this is as finely equipped a studio as the State can show, premises comprising two floors, 100 × 40 and 20 × 40 respectively, are occupied, consisting of operating, reception and printing rooms, etc., and especial facilities are at hand for the doing of large work, to which particular attention is given. Mr. Durgan is a native of Bath, Maine, and has been identified with his present establishment since 1880, but has been thirty-five years in the business. He employs an able corps of assistants, and is prepared to fill all orders at very short notice. Photographs will be made in every style, and copying is done in all its branches. A specialty is made of crayon, India ink, water colors and solar photographs, and the prices quoted are very reasonable when the uniform superiority of the work is considered.

M. A. Potter, Agent, dealer in Fresh and Salt Fish, Oysters, Clams, Canned Goods, Vegetables, Fruits, etc., Main Street, between 6th and 7th Streets, Greeneville, Conn.—Fish is one of the most popular articles of food we have, and it is well that it is so, for it is both cheap and healthful. The only disadvantage connected with the use of it is that it must be perfectly fresh in order to be palatable and nutritious, and there is no difficulty in obtaining perfectly fresh fish if you only know where to look for it. For instance make a call on Mr. M. A. Potter, doing business on Main street between 6th and 7th streets and you will find that his stock of fresh and salt fish, oysters, clams, etc., is full and complete, and that every article sold by him is guaranteed to be satisfactory and to prove as represented. Mr. Potter is a native of Norwich, and is at present a councilman. He inaugurated the enterprise to which we have reference in 1879. He has built up a very large and growing business, and is now better prepared than ever before to supply anything in his line, at the lowest market rates, and to give prompt and careful attention to orders. Employment is given to only competent assistants and all customers are assured prompt and courteous service. Canned goods, vegetables, fruits, etc., are largely handled, and all orders will be delivered when promised, and will be accurately and carefully filled.

John F. Sevin, dealer in Fine Groceries, Provisions and Notions, 190 and 192 East Broad Street, Norwich, Conn.—Mr. J. F. Sevin has been identified with the establishment he now conducts for twenty one years, and he has gained a high and well deserved reputation for handling strictly reliable articles and quoting the lowest market rates in every department of his business. The premises are centrally located and spacious, but none too much so to properly accommodate the heavy stock carried, which comprises groceries, flour, teas, coffees and spices, and other commodities in general use. Mr. Sevin enjoys a large family trade and naturally caters expressly to that class of patrons. The assortment of staple and fancy groceries offered by this firm includes everything in that line in common use, and as the goods are without exception obtained from the most reputable sources, they may be confidently depended on to prove just as represented. Special inducements are given to purchasers of flour, the most popular brands being quoted at bottom prices, and the teas and coffees offered are also sure to give satisfaction, both as regards their quality and their cost. Employment is given to a competent force of assistants, and callers are sure of receiving immediate and courteous attention at all times.

Fred L. Ramage, dealer in Meats, Vegetables and Canned Goods, 19 Ann Street, Norwich, Conn.—Mr. Ramage is a native of Norwich, and established his meat market in 1887. The store contains a well selected stock of fresh and salt meats, beef, pork, mutton, lamb, veal, canned goods, etc. Also vegetables in their seasons. The prices quoted are always in accordance with the lowest market rates, and as the goods are of excellent quality and customers are promptly and politely attended to, it is perfectly natural that a large and growing business should be done. Lack of space forbids our giving the goods constituting his stock the detailed mention their merits deserve, but no doubt the majority of our readers residing in Norwich need not be told that he faithfully carries out the policy of giving every customer the full worth of his money.

Jacob C. Benjamin, Ice Cream Manufacturer. Ladies' and Gents' Dining Saloon; Parties furnished with every Requisite; 14 Broadway, Norwich, Conn.—The residents of Norwich may well take pride in the dining saloon conducted by Mr. Jacob C. Benjamin, at No. 14 Broadway, for there are very few dining-rooms in the State that can compare with this in the various points which go to make up a first class establishment of the kind. Mr. Benjamin is a native of the island of St. Helena, and inaugurated his present enterprise in 1871. He is a caterer of long and varied experience and enjoys facilities which enable him to fill all orders at short notice and in a satisfactory style.

Reiss & Wholey, successors to Myron Sears, dealers in Stoves, Ranges, Tin, Iron and Granite Ware. Tin Roofing, Plumbing and Jobbing promptly attended to. Ordered Work a specialty. No. 12 Ferry Street, Norwich, Conn.— The firm of Reiss & Wholey began operations in 1888, but the business carried on by them is of very old establishment, having been founded many years ago by Mr. H. I. Roath, who was succeeded by Messrs. Roath & Denison, this firm giving place to Messrs. Roath & Bates, and they to Messrs. Roath & Sears, Mr. Myron P. Sears assuming sole control in 1869 and continuing it until succeeded by the present proprietors. Mr. James W. Reiss is a native of Brooklyn, N. Y., and Mr. Andrew J. Wholey of Montville, Conn., and both these gentlemen are well prepared to maintain the honorable repute of the establishment, for they understand their business thoroughly and are enterprising and straightforward in their business methods. The premises made use of are located at No. 12 Ferry street, and comprise three floors, measuring 40×50 feet, thus affording ample opportunity for the carrying of an exceptionally large and varied stock of stoves, ranges, furnaces, tin, iron and granite ware, kitchen furnishings, plumbers' materials, etc. The firm warrant every article they sell to prove just as represented, and are in a position to quote the lowest market rates on all the commodities handled. Ordered work is made a specialty, and tin roofing, plumbing and general jobbing will be done in first-class style at moderate rates.

TWO POPULAR HOTELS.

Crocker House, Hale & Co., Proprietors, New London. —It is not at all difficult to define the position held by the Crocker House among other Connecticut hotels, for this famous hostelry has for years been "the leader of the leaders," and is not out-classed by any hotel in all New England. It is pleasantly familiar to hundreds of the traveling public, and it is safe to say that among the most pleasant remembrances held by a large proportion of those who annually visit New London at the time of the college races, those associated with the Crocker House are by no means to be left out of the account. This hotel is the centre of excitement on such occasions, and one is not at all apt to forget the scenes following the winning of a race by either Yale's or Harvard's representatives. The building is one of the most attractive and substantial in the city; being constructed of brick with granite trimmings, and comprising five floors of the dimensions of 180 × 110 feet. It was erected in 1872, by Mr. S. H. Crocker, and continued under his management for about a year; after several changes in its management the present proprietors, Messrs. A. R. and A. T. Hale, assumed control in 1881. The senior partner is also the owner and manager of the celebrated Watch Hill House, of Watch Hill, R. I., and that they fully appreciate the wants of the public and are competent and determined to cater to those wants in a thoroughly satisfactory manner, the leading position held by both their houses amply proves. The interior appointments of the Crocker House are, like everything else connected with that establishment, strictly first class; the furniture being tasteful and elegant and all the modern improvements, including steam heat, electric bells, electric lights, elevator, etc., being utilized. The dining hall will seat 250 guests, and there are 150 sleeping rooms on the premises. The *cuisine* of the Crocker House has always been one of its strong points, and the accommodations offered at this house are first class in every respect.

Watch Hill House, Watch Hill, R. I.—The attractions of Watch Hill have come to be generally recognized, and the grand beauty of its coast line is attracting summer sojourners from all over the country. Not alone the love for the beautiful is gratified, but the bodily health is benefitted as well, for the cooling ocean breezes bring strength, and the opportunities for driving, fishing, bathing and other inspiriting exercises, are too tempting to be resisted. Notably so in its combination of beautiful ocean and inland scenery. Its beach is conceded to be the finest on the coast, and the surf, while wild and impressive, being particularly suitable for the use of bathers—a fact that hundreds take advantage of daily. Beautiful drives over fine roads are an additional attraction, and the crowning inducement—a first-class hotel—is not wanting, for the "Watch Hill House" is clearly entitled to such a description by the record it has made since its opening. This famous hotel may well be taken as a representative house, for in the opinion of competent observers, it is as near perfection as any similar enterprise on the coast. Accommodations are provided for 300 guests, and the location of the house is well described by its name, it being literally a "sea shore" house, facing on the ocean, and considered the best location on the bill. The bathing beach and the other hotels are within easy walking distance. The fine table is not the least attractive feature and is managed with liberality and intelligence. A number of first class cooks, under a competent *chef*, prepare a very attractive bill of fare, while the service is all that could be desired. The fine music affords every opportunity for dancing. Mr. A. R. Hale, the proprietor, is one of the best-known landlords in New England, and is looked upon as an authority on hotel-keeping matters.

GENERAL BUSINESS AGENCY.

FIRE, LIFE AND ACCIDENT INSURAN

Bills and Rents Collected, Real Estate bought, sold and managed.

NOTARY PUBLIC.

J. W. HARTSHORN,

P. O. Box 943.   No. 3 Bank St. (with Postal Telegraph). New Lc

☞ Agent for Building, Loan and Saving Association of Geneva, N. Y. Authorized capital $5,000,000.

PUTNAM FURNITURE COMPAN

126, 128, 130 BANK STREET, NEW LONDON.

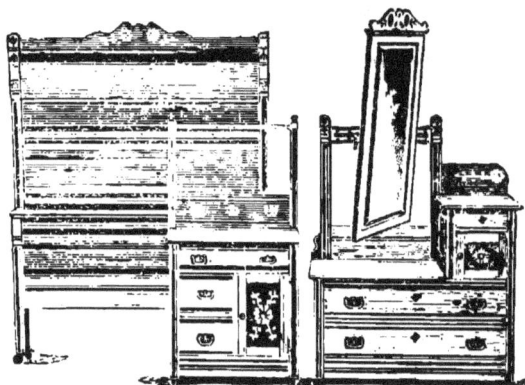

It is said that "Different people have different tastes," and as they also have different incomes, the only practically satisfactory way to cater to all classes of trade, is to carry a stock so large and so varied that it comprises all grades, all styles and all kinds of really meritorious goods. Such is the policy pursued by the Putnam Furniture Manufacturing Company, and that it meets with the favor of the public, is shown by the immense business built up since operations were begun in July, 1889. The company utilize the New London Opera House building, 126-130 Bank street, and have at their disposal, show rooms double the size of any others in the State. The capacity of these rooms is well tested, and those who want *anything* in the line of housekeeping goods, will make a big mistake if they don't at least make this establishment a call. Inspection costs nothing; callers being politely received and no one being importuned to buy, and we can assure ers that a great deal can be learned in the cour hour's visit to this well-managed store. High-co medium cost goods, and low cost goods are all w sented, and the prices quoted are as low as the every time. Goods will be sold for cash or on we ments, and the employment of six competent t assures prompt and polite attention to every caller. will be made to order or repaired at short notice, being spared to satisfy the most critical. The hea worthy enterprise is Mr. Nelson S. Putnam, a r Newton, Mass., and Geo. N. Putnam, the m: native of Boston, and a member of the Odd Fellc is an experienced and energetic man of business, be congratulated on the grand success the underta won.

www.ingramcontent.com/pod-product-compliance
Lightning Source LLC
Chambersburg PA
CBHW031455270326
41930CB00007B/1012